John McLemore's
"DADGUM That's Good!"™

Kickbutt Recipes for Smoking, Grilling, Frying, Boiling and Steaming

John McLemore

Published by Concept, Inc.

First paperback edition 2010

Author: John McLemore
with Concept, Inc. Creative Team

Book Design and Food Photography by Concept, Inc.
John McLemore's Front Cover Photo by Alicia McGlamory

Printed in Canada

ISBN 978-0-578-05954-952495

Left:
Paula Deen and John

Right:
Jamie Deen,
Paula Deen and
John McLemore

Foreword

I'm tickled pink that John has written this cookbook. I can't think of anyone or anything that has made my cooking life easier than John's awesome Masterbuilt products—this is a man who knows how good food should taste and how it's best prepared!

I met John when we were on QVC the same day—John was promoting his products and I had a new book out. Both being devout "foodies," we hit it off immediately and for many years since that meeting I have enjoyed using his Electric Grill and his wonderful Indoor Electric Turkey Fryer in our kitchen in Savannah. I like to do a Southern Low Country Boil in the Turkey Fryer just as much as I love to deep fry our holiday turkeys in it.

John came to our house for a visit not long ago and cooked smoked prime rib and chicken for the family. Sugar, I tell you that was good eatin'! John has set a new standard of cooking with this book, a wonderful collection of more than 125 recipes that are designed specially to be prepared using his equipment—and the results are fantastic. Whether it involves smoking, steaming, frying, or grilling, you can be sure these dishes will have you saying, *"Dadgum That's GOOD!"*

— Paula Deen

Table of Contents

SIGNATURE RECIPES

See pages 23, 29, 33, 37, 67, 89, 95, 105, 117,
121, 123, 129, 147, 167, 185 and 191

Introduction

Left:
Don and John
show off three
signature recipes

Above:
Lynne, Don, John
and Tonya enjoy
lunch at the lake

"DADGUM, That's Good!"™ is much more than just a Southern phrase and the title of this cookbook. It's the summation of a life's work in creating delicious food with our world-class cooking products. For almost 40 years, my brother Don and I have worked together at our family-owned business– Masterbuilt. We have traveled all over the world to demonstrate our cooking products and learned a lot of lessons about food, and life, along the way. Everywhere we go, we have requests for recipes, tips and secrets for our meals. What follows are 128 of those recipes and an abundant supply of tips and secret techniques. We also share our story and hope you will enjoy reading about how our backyard business turned into so much more. In fact, we're bringing what started in our backyard to your table, where we are sure you'll say, *"DADGUM, That's Good!"*

Selecting Cuts of Meat and Seafood

Tips for selecting and preparing

MEAT

Here are some of the cuts of meat most commonly used.

Filet Mignon – Cut from the tenderloin, filet is a very tender cut, but lacks the beefy flavor of other cuts. Consider grilling this with a good rub or marinade.

Flank Steak – A beefy, full-flavored steak cut from the chest and side, this steak is thin and cooks quickly. To retain the juices in the meat, let it rest it for a few minutes before carving against the grain.

Ribeye Steak – Cut from the rib, they are very tender, beefy and well-marbled with fat, which makes them great for grilling and smoking. They should be thick and seared over a medium-high heat. Move to a cooler spot on the grill to finish.

Sirloin, New York Strip and Prime Rib – Full-flavored premium cuts that have a natural flavor, which you may want to bring out with a little salt, pepper, and olive oil.

Porterhouse (T-Bone) – Cut extra thick, this gives you the taste and texture of the strip or the tenderloin. To prevent it from overcooking, sear the steaks with the strip portion facing the hottest part of the fire and the tenderloins facing the cooler side.

Brisket – The brisket consists of two different muscles. The top muscle, known as the "point," is fibrous and difficult to cut. The flat is leaner and more even, which makes it easier to cut. It's likely that you'll find the second cut in your local supermarket, trimmed with a thin layer of fat on the top. If it's untrimmed, trim the fat down to ¼-inch thickness. To test your brisket for tenderness, hold the middle of the brisket in your hand. If the ends give, you've picked the right one. A rigid brisket is a sign that you're in for a tough time.

Spare Ribs – Pick ribs that are between 2 to 4 lbs. Smaller ribs are likely to come from a younger animal and will cook faster because they're more tender.

St. Louis Style Ribs – These specially-trimmed ribs are lighter than spare ribs, topping out at about 2 pounds.

Baby Back Ribs – These flavorsome ribs are great if you're smoking for the first time. Baby Backs are a little more expensive, but they're the most tender and cook faster than spare ribs.

Pork Butts and Picnics – Similar cuts with different bones. There is not much difference between them, but they do offer a choice. You can remove the bone or cook them bone-in.

TIP

Meat cooked on the bone shrinks less. It also allows you to quickly test for tenderness. When the meat is ready, the bone slides out easily. Buy your butt with the fat on and trim it to suit your taste. And remember, fat equals flavor.

Sausages – Simple to grill, and if you're smoking sausage, remove the casing; it blocks smoke from penetrating the meat.

FISH

Mahi-Mahi – Similar in texture to swordfish, but it's a little oilier. Despite this, it dries out quickly on the grill, so you might want to brine it.

Red Snapper – Quick and easy to grill or fry. If you grill, handle carefully. Make sure the fish and the grill are well-oiled.

Salmon – A favorite for grilling because it doesn't dry out. It's rich in healthy, natural oils and fats, so you can pop it on the grill without oiling. Its flavor also complements stronger marinades.

Scallops – You'll want to use fresh ocean scallops if you're grilling or frying them. Take a close look at the scallops before you buy them. If they're unnaturally white and are sitting in a milky liquid, they're processed. Natural scallops are a pinkish tan or ivory. They have a firmer texture and a bigger surface area that holds the batter better.

Trout – Freshwater trout is great on the grill. The skin becomes thin and crispy and the flesh is flavorsome without an overpowering fishiness.

Tuna – Does best using a simple marinade of herbs and oil. This prevents it from drying out and getting tough. If you like your tuna rare, buy 1 ½-inch thick steaks. This will enable you to sear them without overcooking them.

TIP

Fish smokes fast, so it requires a little more attention. The best types of fish to test in your smoker are salmon and trout filets. Boneless fish filets are the easiest to smoke. Fish with a higher fat content, such as trout, salmon, tuna and mackerel, retain their moisture better during smoking. Most fish should be brined and air-dried before smoking.

SEAFOOD

Mussels – Versatile, quick and cheap. They steam beautifully and within minutes you can rustle up a satisfying gourmet dish.

Shrimp – Tastes great any way you cook it. Though some prefer boiled shrimp, there's a lot to be said for steaming them. It retains the delicate flavor better.

USDA* Safe Minimum Internal Temperatures

Fish	145° F
Pork	160° F
Egg Dishes	160° F
Steaks and Roasts of Beef, Veal of Lamb	145° F
Whole Poultry (Turkey, Chicken, Duck, etc.)	165° F
Ground or Pieces Poultry (Chicken Breast, etc.)	165° F

Pantry Essentials

Almonds

Balsamic Vinegar

Bay Leaf

Breadcrumbs

Butterball® Buttery Creole Turkey Marinade

Butterball® Cajun Turkey Seasoning

Capers

Cardamom

Cayenne Pepper

Celery Seed

Chicken Bouillon Cube

Chicken Broth

Chili Powder

Cinnamon-ground, stick

Cloves, ground

Cocoa Powder

Confectioners' Sugar

Coriander

Cornmeal

Cornstarch

Creole Mustard

Cumin, ground

Currants, dried

Curry Powder

Dark Brown Sugar

Dill Weed, dry

Dry Mustard

Extra Virgin Olive Oil

Fennel Seeds

Fish Sauce

Garlic-minced, powder, salt, cloves

Ginger-ground, grated, minced, peeled

Greek Seasoning

Honey

Horseradish

Hot Pepper Flakes

Hot Pepper Sauce

Light Brown Sugar

Light Corn Syrup

Maple Syrup

Nutmeg

Onion Powder

Oregano

Panko (Japanese-style breadcrumbs)

Paprika

Pepper

Peppercorns

Rice Vinegar

Rosemary

Salt

Self-Rising Flour

Sesame Oil, dark

Sesame Seeds

Soy Sauce

Spice Island Chili Powder

Sugar

Thyme

Tomato Paste

Turmeric

Vanilla Extract

Wine Vinegar

Worcestershire Sauce

Yeast, active dry

The Masterbuilt Story
as told by John McLemore

When I was eight-years-old, my brother Don and I arrived home from school and found our dad, Dawson, bending a piece of raw steel with his bare hands. We watched in amazement as he twisted the steel into scrolls and circles that he then welded together to forge a plant stand—his first product.

Neither of us realized then that this was the start of a family business that would ultimately create some of the world's most user-friendly products and cooking equipment.

We were a close-knit family, living in Columbus, Georgia. Mom, Dad and five kids—Bubba, the oldest; then Bill; the twins, Don and Donna; and I was the youngest of the bunch.

Back then, we struggled to get by and we were happy to make a living any which way we could. Dad held a day job with Goodyear Tire and Rubber Company, but by night he'd work on his dream of building a family business. Dad always led by example and never had to tell us what to do. We watched him hard at work and, without even thinking twice, Don and I would roll up our sleeves and pitch in, along with our older brothers, Bill and Bubba.

Donna decided to do other things. To her, getting dirty in the backyard didn't seem like much fun. Momma worked full-time at a local car dealership and ran a busy household with five kids—and a highly motivated husband. She also pitched in when needed, working alongside her boys, and was never afraid to show us how things needed to be done.

While other kids were out playing ball or delivering papers, Don and I always felt we were building something bigger. It wasn't long before our family business—known as M&M Welding—blossomed in the backyard. And it *was* literally in our backyard—on a dirt floor under a tin shed.

Top:
1978, Mom and Dad hug after a great week

Bottom Left:
Dawson while working at Goodyear

Bottom Right:
John takes to the phone early

As the plant stands came off the backyard assembly line, I would load up my Red Ryder wagon with as many as I could cart around the neighborhood. Our neighbors got a real kick out of seeing this scrawny eight-year-old appear on their front doorstep to sell plant stands.

Demand grew, so we all started working longer hours. We would come home from school and head straight to the workshop, stopping only for dinner. Dad would load up his truck and hit the road, selling his wares to nurseries, hardware stores, "mom and pop" general stores—anyone who'd give him the time of day.

Our mom, Evelyn, was a pillar of strength, nurturing our family dream with a steady stream of prayers and encouragement. She would cook dinners that were to die for, especially her Southern fried chicken and homemade biscuits. Her love for great food has been passed on to us and seasons the many great recipes in this book.

All the credit for our achievements has to go to our parents. Without Dad, there would have been no M&M Welding. Without Momma, we'd never have developed our taste for excellent food. Dad's hard work and Momma's culinary skills, together, were instrumental in helping us develop great products and *Dadgum Good* food.

Though we lived modestly, Dad always dreamed up ways to make our family vacations fun. We would all pile into the old pickup truck and haul our inner tubes—borrowed from the Goodyear store, of course—and all the fishing gear, masks and snorkels we owned, and head off to the North Georgia mountains or the Florida springs. We'd float down the river all day and emerge from the freezing water, blue and famished. Dad would fire up the grill and cook burgers and hot dogs for us kids. We always caught so many fish, we never knew what to do with all of them. And that's what got Dad thinking.

Top Left:
Dawson McLemore
Top Middle:
1970, Donna, John and Don with Santa
Top Right:
John at age 6
Below:
Don at age 6

In addition to his reputation as an inventor, Dad was renowned for his fried fish recipe (page 37)—something that went down well after a day of North Georgia whitewater tubing, or spear fishing in the Florida springs. So, the idea for a fish fryer was born. There were no formal drawings, just ideas sketched on paper napkins. Dad secretly worked on it and then presented his new invention to Momma. It was round and very bulky, like a sci-fi spaceship, and the fish we cooked in it were definitely out of this world.

We started hosting regular fish fries with all the fish we brought home. Dad's fried fish was a huge hit—crisp on the outside, light and flaky on the inside, and better than any restaurant's fried fish.

A friend who tasted Dad's fish asked for one of the fish fryers, so Dad built another and traded it for a lawnmower. Word of the invention spread and soon barter turned to buying. For years, all five of us built a few fish fryers every week, tinkering with the design a little bit over time.

Whether by accident or intent, the most important family business principle was born. Every product was designed for our personal use and tested using family recipes. If the fish was good enough for the family, it was good enough for the rest of the world.

Of course, there were many accidents along the way. At age thirteen, while I was grinding a fish cooker pan, I got into a tangle with a large, hand-held grinding machine and came off second best. One hundred and ten stitches and several pints of blood later, I was back in business. I had a good time telling stories of the gruesome details of my accident. Weeks later, when I ran into my friends at the beach, the fresh scars fueled some pretty tall tales—many that included sharks and bears, not a grinding machine. It just sounded cooler.

Above:
Masterbuilt's 1st round-shaped fish cooker

Bottom Left:
John kisses a fish during an ESPN show

Bottom Right:
Dad and Mom fishing on their honeymoon (seated far left)

Nothing would keep our family from realizing the dream that had captured our imaginations. Monday through Friday, Dad would visit every retailer who'd bought plant stands in the past and who might consider purchasing a fish fryer in the future. He'd pull into the parking lot and sell them off the back of his truck. Soon, single orders turned to dozens. Dad would arrive with a baker's dozen—a "buy-12-get-one-free" deal. He never had a problem unloading that extra fryer and his products were becoming wildly popular.

As demand grew, imitators sprang up, yet we always managed to stay one step ahead, leading the pack with innovation and product improvements that would separate us from our competitors. It was as if Dad's constant quest for different and better had been baked into our company's DNA.

That quest for the best prompted us to add an aluminum pan to the fish fryer, causing sales to skyrocket. At that time, our little backyard company, M&M Welding, was the only company building a fish fryer with an aluminum pan. Dad never copied anyone else's ideas. And the only person we kids ever copied was Dad.

In 1976, as sales grew, Dad left Goodyear to focus on the family business. He had all four boys solidly behind him, but still felt he could never go it alone. In 1978, we abandoned the name "M&M Welding" and renamed the company "Masterbuilt." This reflected our belief that we needed the support of the Lord, our "Master," combined with the fact that we "built" products. So there you have it, the name "Masterbuilt" was created.

Continued on page 18

Left:
Hanging out at the lake

Top Right:
John with his sister Donna and friends shucking corn

Right:
John cooking fish at camp

Bottom Right:
John and Don in Mexico filming an ESPN show

Alabama BBQ Sauce

Kansas City Classic Sauce

Memphis Sweet & Hot BBQ Sauce

You'll Need:
- 1 cup mayonnaise
- 1 cup cider vinegar
- 1 tablespoon lemon juice
- 1 tablespoon black pepper
- ½ teaspoon salt
- ½ teaspoon cayenne pepper

1. Mix mayonnaise, vinegar, lemon juice, black pepper, salt, and cayenne pepper together. Refrigerate for at least 8 hours before using. Brush lightly over chicken, turkey or pork during the last few minutes of grilling or smoking.

You'll Need:
- ¼ teaspoon allspice
- ¼ teaspoon mace
- ¼ teaspoon black pepper
- ½ teaspoon curry powder
- ¼ teaspoon cinnamon
- ½ teaspoon chili powder
- ½ teaspoon paprika
- ¼ cup white vinegar
- 1 teaspoon hot pepper sauce
- 1 cup ketchup
- ⅓ cup dark molasses

1. Mix allspice, mace, pepper, curry powder, cinnamon, chili powder, and paprika in a large mixing bowl. Stir in vinegar, pepper sauce, ketchup, and molasses and thoroughly mix until blended. Serve this sauce at room temperature or heated.

You'll Need:
- 2 cups ketchup
- ½ cup yellow mustard
- ½ cup packed brown sugar
- ¼ cup apple cider vinegar
- 1 tablespoon red pepper flakes, to taste
- 1 tablespoon onion powder
- 1 tablespoon chili powder
- 1 tablespoon black pepper
- 2 teaspoons garlic powder
- ½ teaspoon celery salt
- ½ teaspoon salt
- 1 tablespoon liquid smoke
- 3 tablespoons Worcestershire sauce

1. Combine all ingredients in a medium non-reactive saucepan. Bring to a simmer and cook over low heat for 25 minutes, stirring occasionally, until smooth and thickened. Let cool slightly and serve. This BBQ sauce gets better the longer it sits.

Eastern North Carolina Herbed Sauce

You'll Need:

- 1 cup cider vinegar
- ½ cup water
- ⅔ cup onion, minced
- 1 clove garlic, crushed
- 1 teaspoon black pepper
- ½ teaspoon salt
- 2 teaspoons red pepper flakes
- 1 teaspoon sugar
- 1 bay leaf
- ⅔ teaspoon thyme
- 3 tablespoons peanut oil
- 3 teaspoons dry mustard

1. Mix vinegar, water, onion, garlic, black pepper, salt, red pepper flakes, sugar, bay leaf, thyme, peanut oil, and dry mustard in medium saucepan. Boil for 5 minutes.

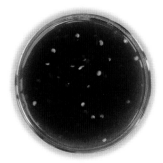

North Carolina BBQ Sauce

You'll Need:

- 2 cups cider vinegar
- 3 cups water
- ½ cup Texas Pete hot sauce
- 1 cup brown sugar, packed
- ½ cup crushed red pepper
- ½ cup molasses
- 1 cup ketchup
- Black pepper

1. Mix vinegar, water, Texas Pete hot sauce, brown sugar, red pepper, molasses, ketchup, and pepper to taste in a large saucepan. Bring to a boil, reduce heat to low and simmer for 1 hour. Pour over cooked and shredded pork; mix well.

South Carolina Mustard Sauce

You'll Need:

- ½ cup cider vinegar
- 6 tablespoons Dijon mustard
- 2 tablespoons honey
- 4 teaspoons Worcestershire sauce
- 1 teaspoon hot red pepper sauce
- 2 tablespoons ketchup
- 1 tablespoon brown sugar
- 2 teaspoons salt
- Black pepper

1. Mix vinegar, mustard, honey, Worcestershire sauce, pepper sauce, ketchup, brown sugar, salt, and pepper to taste, in medium bowl.

The Masterbuilt Story
as told by John McLemore

Don graduated from high school in 1981, and I managed to squeak by in 1983. We both knew that Masterbuilt was where we were destined to work. College for us was, as Don fondly called it, "The University of Masterbuilt." A family-owned university that allowed us to create products to help us cook the great food we all loved so much and wanted to share.

Although I know I would have benefited from a college degree, my work exposed me to hands-on learning that I would never have gained in school. I had direct and constant contact with our customers; I was able to understand their needs and spot product opportunities in a timely manner. While I focused on building a solid sales and management team, Don was instrumental in developing our distribution and handling the logistics.

Don and I have always had a unique partnership. Though we have taken on separate roles at Masterbuilt, we're all about teamwork when it comes to developing innovative ideas. We bounce ideas back and forth until we have a product idea that's truly unique, and a way to grow our business that always keeps family first.

We continued to expand our cooking products into the '80s, and a new turkey fryer we created really took the family by surprise.

It was Thanksgiving, 1982, and I called my mom and told her, "Momma, don't cook a turkey. Don and I have built a turkey fryer and I'd like to deep fry the turkey for the whole family." She probably thought I was nuts. Nobody was deep-frying turkeys back then.

Top:
John's graduation from High School

Below Top:
John at a Masterbuilt trade show

Bottom Left:
Back in 1995, family and friends cheered on John and Don at an exhibition race

Bottom Right:
Don peeks through the turkey basket

Thanksgiving dinner was a duty that usually fell to Momma, so she wasn't eager to leave that responsibility to me. But, Momma agreed. Not one to be thrown off balance, she snapped into action and made a few calls. Nobody in the family was willing to contemplate Thanksgiving without a turkey, so Momma arranged—without my knowledge—for a family member to bring a back-up, oven-baked turkey, just in case.

At 4:30 p.m. on the big day, I showed up armed with the new turkey fryer and a raw turkey. A little after 5:45 p.m., a crisp, golden brown deep-fried turkey graced the table. Heavenly scented, succulent and moist on the inside, it was unlike anything our family had ever seen or tasted.

With one bite, doubts about our newfangled turkey fryer evaporated. The turkey was picked clean. It was Don who finally broke the silence that came over the table when he said, "John, if I have heard you say it once, I've heard you say it a thousand times, *"Dadgum, That's Good!"*

Nobody disagreed. And the ladies of our family graciously admitted that no back-up turkey would ever be needed again. To this day, our deep fried turkey is still the centerpiece on the McLemore Thanksgiving table, and our recipe is still prepared and enjoyed by the whole family (see page 23.)

Don and I have never built a product that didn't stand up to the stringent standards set by our family— nor would we ever. In creating the Turkey Fryer, Dad decided that Don and I were ready to take the reins of the company and he opted for semi-retirement in 1984.

Don took on plant operations, while I handled sales. Masterbuilt's goals and vision seemed set, but Don and I knew we would need help if we were to grow the company. In 1988, Bill decided to go out on his own and start farming. Later in 1997, Bubba, who led our trailer division, left Masterbuilt and joined forces with Bill to continue manufacturing and successfully selling MasteRyde trailers.

Then fate intervened in the form of Tonya and Lynne...

Top Left:
John and Don cooking at a NASCAR race

Top Right:
John and Don with former NASCAR champion, Cale Yarborough

Bottom:
John and Don film a commercial with the late great NASCAR driver, Davey Allison

Continued on page 100

"I believe I can fry!"

Recipes for the best deep-fryer in the world.

The Butterball® Indoor Electric Turkey Fryer and the Masterbuilt All-Purpose Fryer help you to overcome your fear of frying. Its patented technology makes your fryer safe and guarantees you will never over-heat your oil.

- There's no open flame to worry about. It's the fastest way to serve up the best turkey you'll ever taste, in three easy steps: inject, fry and eat.

- All recipes were tested in the Butterball Indoor Electric Turkey Fryer or Masterbuilt All-Purpose Fryer. Note: Masterbuilt also sells a Butterball® XL Model Fryer, which fries up to a 20 lb. turkey and requires 3 gallons of cooking oil.

TIPS

- Our Butterball Indoor Electric Turkey Fryer is the best out there, but don't let the name fool you. This unit also steams and boils. So, whether you are in the mood to indulge in some fried food, or you're being a bit more health-conscious, we've got you covered.

- Anytime you cook with hot oil or water, safety needs to take top priority. Never leave unit unattended while cooking.

- There are many cooking oils to choose from. We recommend peanut oil. Not only is it known for its flavor, it's also a healthier, more robust oil that lasts longer.

- Many people ask us, "How many times can I use my oil?" The drain valve on our turkey fryer makes for quick and easy clean-up and allows you to re-use your oil 6 or 8 times. Oil breakdown will occur depending on the amount of seasonings used. Straining the oil of sediments after each use prolongs its life. Store it in a cool place and if the oil gets too dark in color, it's time to change.

- When frying, boiling, or steaming, always use caution and wear protective gloves. Be sure to keep the lid closed, which will keep the heat and/or steam in the unit.

"NEVER place a frozen turkey in hot oil.
Never leave a fryer unattended."

Cajun Deep-Fried Turkey
and Buffalo Sauce

Serves 6 to 12

1. Thaw turkey, if frozen. To properly thaw a frozen turkey in the refrigerator allow approximately 24 hours for every 4 pounds. Fill Butterball® Indoor Electric Turkey Fryer with oil to the MAX line; heat to 375° F. Remove giblets and neck. If present, remove and discard plastic leg holder and pop-up timer. Rinse turkey thoroughly with warm water or completely cover with warm water and soak for no more than 30 minutes to ensure cavities are free of ice.

2. Pat turkey completely dry on outside and inside of cavity with paper towels. Using an injector syringe, inject ½ cup (4 ounces) Butterball® Buttery Creole Marinade in each breast. Inject ¼ cup (2 ounces) marinade into each leg and thigh. Sprinkle turkey generously with Butterball® Cajun Turkey Seasoning, completely coating the outside of the turkey and inside of the cavity.

3. Place turkey breast side up in fryer basket. Slowly lower the basket into hot oil, being careful not to splatter hot oil. Fry turkey for 3 ½ to 4 minutes per pound. Lift the basket from the hot oil slowly, hooking the basket's drain clip into drain clip mounting hole to stabilize as you check doneness. Insert a meat thermometer in the meaty part of the breast; turkey is done when it reads 165° F. If the turkey is not done, lower it carefully back into the oil for an additional 5 minutes. Once the turkey reaches the desired temperature (minimum 165° F), turn the turkey fryer to MIN and unplug it from the outlet.

4. Allow the turkey to rest and drain in the fryer basket for 10 minutes before removing for carving. The turkey can remain in the basket to cool until ready to serve.

Sauce:

1. In a medium saucepan, combine hot sauce, butter, garlic powder, and lime juice, and heat over low heat.

2. Use as a dipping sauce or pour over turkey slices.

You'll Need:
- 10 to 14 lbs. fresh or frozen turkey
- 2 gallons cooking oil, preferably peanut oil
- 1 (16 ounce) bottle Butterball Buttery Creole Turkey Marinade
- Butterball Cajun Turkey Seasoning

Sauce:
- 1 (10 to 12 ounce) bottle of your favorite hot sauce
- ½ stick butter (¼ cup)
- ¼ teaspoon garlic powder
- 1 ½ teaspoons freshly-squeezed lime juice

JOHN says

Frying a turkey in hot oil calls for a cool head and a fair measure of caution. Fortunately, Masterbuilt developed the Butterball Indoor Electric Turkey Fryer so you can perfect this great recipe with peace of mind. You want to start with a turkey that's fully thawed and dry; oil and water do not mix. Just follow the safety instructions included in the operation manual closely and you'll fry a turkey so good, you'll never want to roast one in the oven again.

Cajun Fish and Chips

Serves 4

You'll Need:
- 1 gallon cooking oil
- 1 cup all-purpose flour
- 2 tablespoons Butterball Cajun Seasoning
- 1 cup club soda
- 1 ¼ teaspoons salt
- ¼ teaspoon black pepper
- 1 ½ lbs. cod filets (¾-inch thick), cut crosswise into 2-inch wide strips
- 2 lbs. russet potatoes, peeled and sliced into ½-inch wide strips
- Malt vinegar
- Lemon wedges

1. Fill Butterball® or Masterbuilt Fryer with oil. Heat to 375° F; this will take approximately 15 to 20 minutes.

2. Add potatoes and fry until golden brown, about 8 minutes, stirring often. Lift the basket of fries slowly out of the oil and transfer to paper towels to drain. Sprinkle with ½ teaspoon salt.

3. Whisk flour and club soda in a medium bowl until it forms a smooth batter.

4. Sprinkle fish with ½ teaspoon salt, ¼ teaspoon pepper, and Cajun seasoning. Coat fish in batter and fry until coating is crisp and golden brown, and the fish is opaque, about 5 to 6 minutes. Transfer fish to paper towels and sprinkle with ¼ teaspoon salt. Serve with vinegar and lemon wedges.

JOHN *says*

Frying fish is a great option for entertaining large groups of people, because catfish and cod are fairly inexpensive. Fried fish cooks quickly and holds together well, making it ideal for buffet-style gatherings. Make sure that your oil reaches 375° F before you add the fish. If you add it too soon you'll get soggy, greasy fish.

Spicy-Hot Fried Chicken

Serves 4 to 6

1. In a medium bowl, slightly beat the egg, then add hot sauce, and whisk together thoroughly. Set aside. In a separate large bowl, add flour and set aside.

2. Fill Butterball® or Masterbuilt Fryer with oil. Heat to 375° F; this will take approximately 15 to 20 minutes.

3. Wash chicken, dry and sprinkle with the Cajun seasoning. Dip chicken in egg/sauce mixture, then in flour, coating thoroughly. Place chicken on a cooling rack until the flour completely absorbs egg mixture, about 5 minutes.

4. Add chicken to fryer basket and fry for 12 to 15 minutes at 375° F, until golden brown. Drain chicken on rack, and serve.

You'll Need:

- 1 egg
- 1 cup hot sauce (brand and heat of your choice)
- ½ cup flour
- 1 gallon cooking oil
- 1 whole chicken, cut up, or your favorite pieces
- Cajun seasoning

JOHN says

Flour only a couple of pieces of chicken at a time so that each piece gets completely coated and the flour is not gummy. If you want to kick up the spice, add 1 tablespoon of the Butterball® Cajun Seasoning to the flour.

Deep-Fried Catfish
in a Mustard Cornmeal Batter
Serves 2 to 4

1. Fill Butterball® or Masterbuilt Fryer with oil. Heat to 375° F; this will take approximately 15 to 20 minutes.

2. Mix the cornmeal, paprika, salt, and pepper in a shallow dish. In three separate dishes, put the flour, mustard, and cornmeal for dredging.

3. Pat the catfish filets dry and dredge each in flour. Next, roll the filets in the mustard to coat, and then dredge in the seasoned cornmeal mixture. Deep fry until golden brown and crispy, approximately 4 minutes each side.

You'll Need:
- 1 gallon cooking oil
- 2 cups cornmeal
- 1 tablespoon paprika
- 1 teaspoon salt
- 1 teaspoon black pepper
- 2 lbs. catfish filets (about five)
- 1 cup flour
- ½ cup mild deli mustard

JOHN *says*

For a fried fish finger basket, cut the filets into 2 by 4-inch wide strips. Never stack fish on top of each other when frying.

Hawaiian Shrimp Kabobs
with a Sweet Chili Dipping Sauce
Serves 2 to 4

1. Fill Butterball® or Masterbuilt Fryer with oil. Heat to 350° F; this will take approximately 15 to 20 minutes.

2. In a large, shallow dish, mix the flour with the salt. In two separate large, shallow dishes, place shredded coconut and beaten eggs.

3. Thread 3 to 4 shrimp onto each skewer. Roll the skewers in seasoned flour mixture. Then dip the skewers in the beaten egg and dip in shredded coconut, making sure that each shrimp is fully coated.

4. Using the fryer basket, fry the skewers until the shrimp turns golden brown, about 2 to 3 minutes. Remove skewers and drain on paper towels.

Sauce:

1. In a small saucepan, add water and sugar and cook over medium heat, stirring occasionally, for 3 to 5 minutes, until sauce thickens.

2. Stir in the garlic, hot pepper flakes, ginger, cider, and fish sauce. Bring to a boil, then let simmer for 3 minutes.

3. Remove from heat and let sauce cool before serving.

You'll Need:
- 1 gallon cooking oil
- 1 lb. large shrimp (16 to 20 count) cleaned and peeled, leave tail on
- ½ cup all-purpose flour
- ½ teaspoon salt
- 1 ½ cups shredded unsweetened coconut
- 2 eggs beaten with pinch of salt
- 6 wooden skewers, presoaked

Sauce:
- 6 tablespoons sugar
- 2 cloves garlic, minced
- 4 teaspoons hot pepper flakes
- Small piece of ginger, sliced into thin strips
- ½ cup water
- 5 tablespoons cider or rice vinegar
- 1 tablespoon fish sauce

SIGNATURE RECIPE

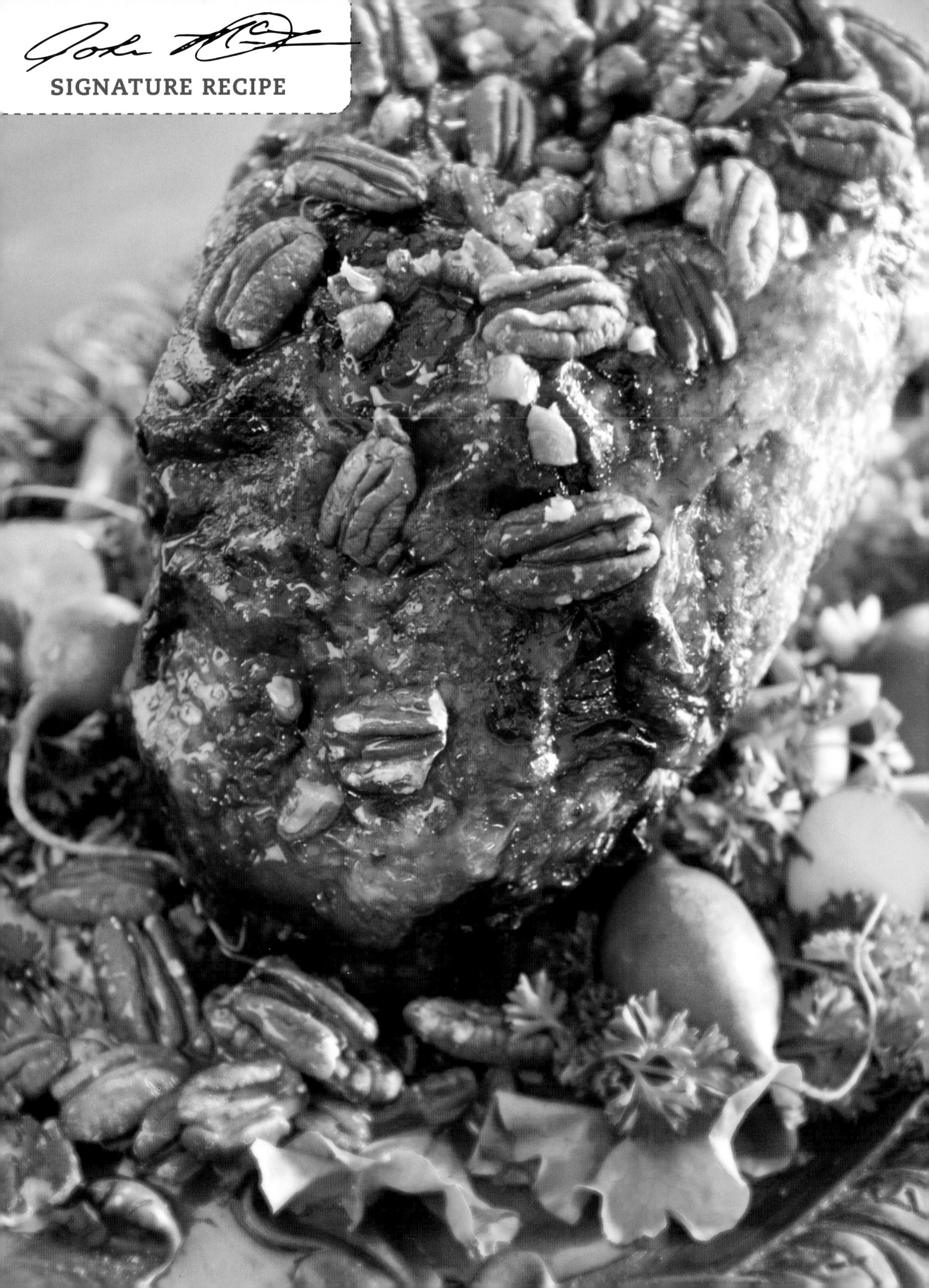

Honey-Glazed Roasted Pecan Deep-Fried Turkey Breast

Serves 6 to 8

1. Fill Butterball® Indoor Electric Turkey Fryer with oil to the MAX line. Heat to 375° F; this will take approximately 20 to 25 minutes.

2. To properly thaw a frozen turkey breast in the refrigerator allow approximately 24 hours for every 4 pounds. If present, remove and discard pop-up timer. Rinse turkey breast thoroughly with warm water, or cover with warm water and soak for no more than 30 minutes to ensure cavities are free of ice. Pat turkey breast completely dry with paper towels, inside and out. Using injector syringe, inject ½ cup (4 ounces) of chicken broth into each side of breast.

3. Place turkey in fryer basket and slowly lower basket into hot oil; be cautious of splattering. Cover and reduce heat to 325° F. Fry turkey breast for 7 minutes per pound. After calculated cooking time is complete, lift the basket from the hot oil slowly, hooking the drain clip of the basket into the drain clip mounting hole. To check doneness, insert a meat thermometer into the meaty part of the breast; it is done when it reads 165° F. If turkey breast is not done, lower it back into the oil for an additional 5 minutes. Repeat basket procedure to check temperature again. Once turkey breast reaches a minimum temperature of 165° F, turn the turkey fryer to MIN and unplug it from the outlet. Allow the turkey breast to rest and drain in the fryer basket for 5 minutes before removing and applying glaze. Carve and serve.

You'll Need:

- 2 gallons peanut oil
- 1 (5 to 7 lb.) turkey breast, bone-in
- 1 cup chicken broth

Pecan Glaze:

- 1 cup pecans, halved
- 1 cup honey
- ¾ cup (1 ½ sticks) butter

Pecan Glaze:

1. Preheat oven to 375° F. Spread pecans in a single layer on a baking sheet. Bake 8 minutes, or until lightly browned. Remove from oven, let cool, and chop coarsely.

2. In a small saucepan over medium-high heat, combine honey and butter. Stir in toasted, chopped pecans and cook for 8 minutes to infuse the flavors. Remove from heat and keep warm.

3. Once turkey breast has rested, place onto a serving platter and pour glaze over top of turkey breast.

JOHN *says*

Although this recipe calls for chopping the pecans, leaving a few of them whole makes for a beautiful presentation. The combination of flavors in this glaze satisfies your sweet and salty cravings. If you can save a little of the glaze, I even like to drizzle it over a scoop of vanilla ice cream for a *Dadgum Good* dessert!

Fried Wontons
with Chipotle Picadillo Filling
Makes 40 pieces

1. Fill Butterball® or Masterbuilt Fryer with oil. Heat to 375° F; this will take approximately 15 to 20 minutes.

2. Cook ground pork in a large skillet over medium heat until it begins to brown, about 5 minutes, stirring to break meat into small pieces. Drain meat and add green onion, raisins, and garlic and continue cooking until meat is done and onion is tender, about 5 more minutes. Remove from heat and stir in Tabasco chipotle sauce, almonds, cinnamon, salt, cumin, and cloves, mixing well.

3. To make wontons, work with a few wraps at a time, keeping remainder covered so they don't dry out. To assemble a wonton dumpling, place the wrapper in the palm of your hand and fill it with a scant teaspoon of the filling (don't overfill!). Brush the edges of the wonton with water and pinch the dumpling closed with your fingers. Make sure the seal is tight so your filling does not ooze out.

4. Fry wontons in fryer basket, a few at a time, until crisp and golden brown, about 3 to 5 minutes. Drain on paper towels and serve hot with salsa.

Salsa:

1. In a medium bowl, mix cream cheese, sour cream, tomatoes, pepper, celery seed, cumin, garlic, cilantro, and lime juice. Use for dipping wontons.

You'll Need:
- 1 lb. lean ground pork
- ½ cup green onions, chopped
- ⅓ cup raisins
- 1 large clove garlic, minced
- 5 tablespoons Tabasco chipotle sauce
- ¼ cup slivered almonds, toasted and chopped
- 1 teaspoon ground cinnamon
- ¾ teaspoon salt
- ¼ teaspoon ground cumin
- ⅛ teaspoon ground cloves
- 1 (12 ounce) package wonton wraps (50 count)
- 1 gallon cooking oil

Salsa:
- 1 (8 ounce) package cream cheese, softened
- 1 tablespoon sour cream
- 1 cup diced tomatoes
- 1 teaspoon black pepper
- 1 teaspoon celery seed
- ½ teaspoon ground cumin
- 2 teaspoons garlic powder
- 1 cup fresh cilantro, chopped
- 1 tablespoon fresh lime juice

JOHN *says*

Working with wonton wrappers may look intimidating, but they're simple and *Dadgum Good!*

MeMaw's Southern Fried Chicken

Serves 4 to 6

1. Fill Butterball® or Masterbuilt Fryer with oil. Heat to 375° F; this will take approximately 15 to 20 minutes.

2. Sprinkle chicken with salt and pepper. Pour the buttermilk into medium bowl. Place the flour in a separate medium-sized bowl. Dip the chicken pieces in buttermilk coating them well, then dredge in the flour.

3. Place the chicken pieces in the fryer and cook for 15 minutes until golden brown. Once the chicken is done, turn the fryer to MIN and unplug it from the outlet. Allow the chicken to drain in fryer basket before removing. Place on paper towels to rest.

You'll Need:
- 1 gallon cooking oil
- 1 (3-lb.) fryer, cut into pieces
- 1 teaspoon salt
- 1 teaspoon black pepper
- 1 cup buttermilk
- 1 ½ cups self-rising flour

JOHN says

Our kids affectionately call my momma "MeMaw." She makes the best *Dadgum* fried chicken... the kind that'll make you slap yourself! Momma would peel the skin off hers and Don and I would fight over it. In fact, in more than 35 years of working together, that's the only thing we've ever fought over!

Deep-Fried Pork Chops
Serves 4

1. Fill Butterball® or Masterbuilt Fryer with oil. Heat to 375° F; this will take approximately 15 to 20 minutes.

2. Pound pork chops with meat tenderizer until ¼-inch thick. Season with salt and pepper to taste and cut into 3-inch pieces.

3. In a shallow dish, whisk together 2 cups flour, 1 teaspoon salt, and 1 teaspoon pepper. In a separate dish, whisk together egg, ¾ cup milk, remaining ¾ teaspoon salt, and remaining ½ teaspoon pepper.

4. Dip pork pieces in egg mixture to coat, then dredge in flour. Transfer coated pork to a large rack with a baking sheet underneath to catch any dripping batter. Let pork stand, uncovered, at room temperature for 15 minutes.

5. Fry pork in batches, turning once, until golden brown, about 4 minutes per batch. Transfer to paper towels to drain. Return oil to 375° F between batches. Keep pork warm on a clean baking sheet in the oven.

6. To make gravy, place 2 tablespoons oil in a large skillet, add the remaining 3 tablespoons flour and cook on moderate heat, stirring constantly for 3 minutes. Slowly whisk in the remaining 2 ½ cups milk and bring to a boil. Reduce heat and simmer, whisking occasionally, about 5 minutes, until gravy thickens. Season with salt and pepper to taste and serve over pork.

You'll Need:
- 1 gallon cooking oil
- 4 (½-inch thick) boneless rib pork chops (1 ½ lbs. total)
- 1 ¾ teaspoon salt
- 1 ½ teaspoon black pepper
- 2 cups, plus 3 tablespoons all-purpose flour
- 1 large egg
- 3 ¼ cups whole milk
- 2 tablespoons vegetable oil

JOHN says

This is comfort food at its best. Our Smoked Cabbage and Mac 'n' Cheese would complete this meal. (See pages 112 and 125 for recipes.) You can also season the gravy by adding a touch of sage.

Deep-Fried Sea Scallops

Serves 2

1. Fill Butterball® or Masterbuilt Fryer with oil. Heat to 375° F; this will take approximately 15 to 20 minutes.

2. Wash scallops; and pat dry with paper towel. In a medium bowl, mix apple juice and scallops; stir well and let stand 15 minutes. Combine cornstarch, salt, and pepper in a small plastic bag. Add several scallops at a time to the bag and shake well to coat. Dip coated scallops in beaten egg, then in breadcrumbs.

3. Carefully place scallops into fryer basket and lower into hot oil. Deep-fry about 6 at a time for approximately 2 to 3 minutes, until golden brown. Remove scallops from basket and drain on paper towels. Serve with your favorite cocktail sauce.

You'll Need:

- 1 gallon cooking oil
- ½ lb. fresh scallops
- 2 teaspoons apple juice, or white grape juice
- ⅓ cup cornstarch
- ½ teaspoon salt
- ¼ teaspoon black pepper
- 1 egg, beaten
- ½ cup fine breadcrumbs

JOHN says

You'll want to use fresh sea scallops for this recipe. Take a close look at the scallops before you buy them. If they're unnaturally white and are packaged in a milky liquid, they're processed; stay away from them. Natural scallops are a pinkish tan or ivory color, not white. They have a firmer texture and a bigger surface area that holds the batter better. Remember, fry them separately, don't fry too many at one time and use a ladle to keep them from touching each other during frying.

SIGNATURE RECIPE

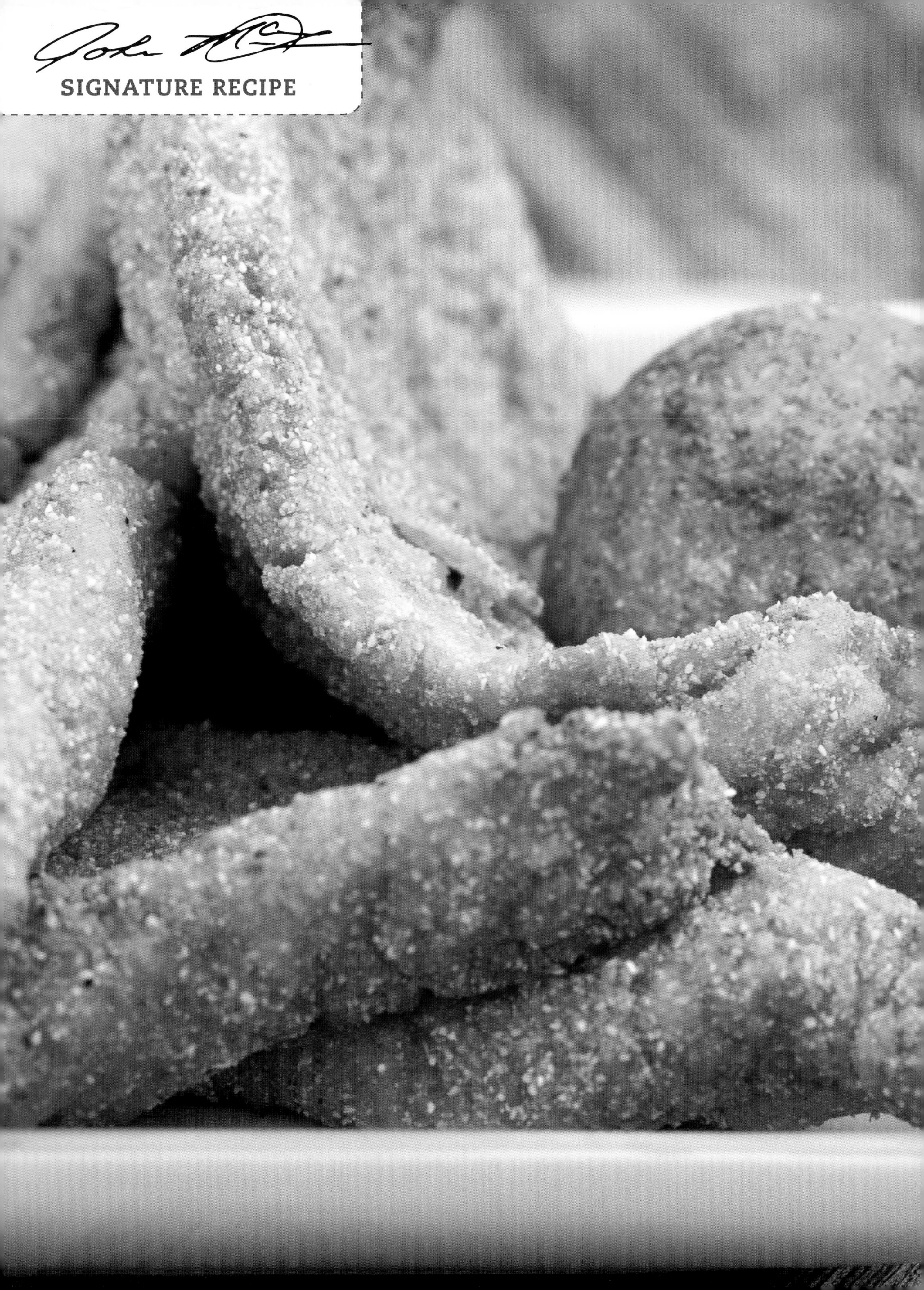

PawPaw's Old Fashioned Southern Fried Fish & Hush Puppies

Serves 6 to 8

1. Fill Butterball® or Masterbuilt Fryer with oil. Heat to 375° F; this will take approximately 15 to 20 minutes.

2. Thaw fish (if frozen). Clean the fish and season with salt. Coat fish with cornmeal. Shaking off any excess coating. Place fish into hot oil and cook for 3 ½ minutes per side. Fish should be golden brown on both sides, crusty on the outside and moist and flaky on the inside. Allow the fish to drain in fryer basket before removing.

Hush Puppies:

1. Combine cornmeal, flour, baking soda, egg, and onions in medium bowl. Stirring, add buttermilk until the consistency is thick enough to form golf ball-sized hush puppies.

2. Drop the batter, 1 tablespoon at a time, into the oil. Dip the spoon in a glass of water to clean it after each hush puppy is dropped into the oil. Fry hush puppies for 4 to 6 minutes, until golden brown, turning the hush puppies during the cooking process to cook evenly. Once the hush puppies are done, turn the turkey fryer to MIN and unplug it from the outlet. Allow the hush puppies to drain in fryer basket before removing.

You'll Need:

- 1 gallon cooking oil
- 4 lbs. fresh or frozen catfish filets or whiting fish (about 24 filets)
- 2 teaspoons salt
- 3 cups cornmeal

Hush Puppies:

- 2 cups yellow cornmeal
- ½ cup self-rising flour
- 1/16 teaspoon baking soda
- 1 large egg, lightly beaten
- ¼ cup yellow onion, chopped
- 1 ½ cups buttermilk

Optional Ingredients for Hush Puppies:

- ¼ cup chopped jalapeño peppers
- ½ cup grated Cheddar cheese
- ½ cup corn

JOHN *says*

My dad, Dawson McLemore ("PawPaw" to my kids), is the founder of Masterbuilt and the "master" of fish frys. Although I have perfected this recipe, make no mistake about it, PawPaw does it best! MeMaw says he stole the hush puppy recipe from her. Hush... we won't tell. Stolen or not, they are *"Dadgum Good!"*

Deep-Fried Macaroni and Cheese

Makes about 20 bars

1. Cook pasta according to package instructions until al dente; don't overcook. Drain in a colander and rinse under running water until slightly cooled. Set aside.

2. Melt butter in a 6-quart pot over medium-high heat. Add flour and mustard and whisk constantly for 5 minutes or until lightly browned. Stir in milk, cream, onion, Andouille, bay leaf, and paprika, then cook, stirring constantly, until sauce thickens (about 5 minutes). Reduce heat and simmer 5 additional minutes.

3. Gradually stir about 1 cup of the sauce into a beaten egg, then add the egg mixture back to remaining sauce in the pot. Add 3 cups cheese, salt, pepper, and hot sauce, stirring until cheese is melted. Remove from heat and stir in the macaroni. Pour into a greased 2-quart rectangular baking dish.

4. To make the topping, combine melted butter and panko in a small bowl. Sprinkle remaining 1 cup cheese evenly over macaroni, then sprinkle with panko mixture. Bake in a 350° F oven for 30 minutes. Let cool completely, then cover and refrigerate overnight.

5. Fill Butterball® or Masterbuilt Fryer with oil. Heat to 350° F; this will take approximately 15 to 20 minutes.

6. Cut the refrigerated casserole lengthwise down the middle, then across into 1-inch bars. For breading, set up three bowls: in the first bowl, combine flour and cayenne; beat eggs in the second bowl; and place panko in the third. Dredge the macaroni bars first in flour, then the egg, then the panko, and place on a baking sheet. Work quickly; don't over-handle. Let bars rest in refrigerator for 20 minutes to set.

7. Fry bars, three at a time for 3 to 4 minutes or until golden brown. Season hot bars with additional salt and pepper. Serve immediately.

You'll Need:

- ½ lb. (1 cup) uncooked elbow macaroni
- 3 tablespoons butter
- 3 tablespoons all-purpose flour
- 1 tablespoon dry mustard
- 2 cups milk
- 1 cup heavy cream
- ½ cup chopped yellow onion
- 1 lb. Andouille sausage (casing removed), diced
- 1 bay leaf
- 1 teaspoon sweet paprika
- 1 large egg, beaten
- 14 ounces (4 cups) sharp white Cheddar cheese, shredded
- 1 teaspoon kosher salt
- 1 teaspoon black pepper
- 2 tablespoons hot sauce
- 3 tablespoons butter
- 1 cup panko (Japanese-style breadcrumbs)

Breading:

- 3 cups all-purpose flour
- 1 teaspoon cayenne pepper
- 5 eggs, beaten
- 2 cups panko (Japanese-style breadcrumbs)
- 1 gallon cooking oil

Fried Fish Tacos

Serves 6

1. Fill Butterball® or Masterbuilt Fryer with oil. Heat to 350° F; this will take approximately 15 to 20 minutes.

2. For the batter, combine 1 cup flour, salt, oregano, dry mustard, garlic salt, and pepper in a large bowl. Using a whisk, stir sparkling water into the flour mixture until well-blended. Set aside.

3. Rinse fish and pat dry with paper towels. Cut filets into 12 (1 by 5-inch) pieces.

4. Place ½ cup flour in shallow bowl. Dredge fish in the flour. Dip fish into batter, taking care to coat all sides. Place about 3 pieces of fish in a single layer in hot oil. Cook in batches of three, about 2 minutes per side or until batter is crispy and golden brown.

Salsa:

1. In a medium bowl, combine tomatoes, onion, jalapeños, cilantro, salt, and lime juice. Refrigerate until ready to serve.

White Sauce:

1. In a small bowl, mix mayonnaise, yogurt, cilantro, and lime juice until blended. Refrigerate until ready to serve.

Serving Instructions:

1. Warm tortillas according to package directions. To assemble, layer a fish filet, white sauce, salsa, avocado, and cabbage on each tortilla. Top with a squeeze of lime. Fold tortilla around ingredients to serve.

JOHN *says*

Most people think of bass as a sport fish you catch and release. Well, Don and I catch and eat them. While down in El Salto, Mexico, we hit the bass jackpot and cooked them every way possible, which is where this taco recipe was created. Bass is great, but you can substitute it with most any white fish.

You'll Need:

- 1 gallon cooking oil
- 1 ½ cups unbleached all-purpose flour
- ½ teaspoon salt
- ½ teaspoon oregano, dried
- ½ teaspoon dry mustard
- ¼ teaspoon garlic salt
- ¼ teaspoon black pepper
- 1 cup sparkling water
- 1 ½ lbs. cod or bass
- 12 fresh stone-ground corn or flour tortillas
- 1 ripe avocado, peeled, pitted and cut into slices
- 3 cups cabbage, finely shredded
- 3 limes, cut into wedges

Salsa:
- 3 cups tomatoes, diced
- ½ cup white onion, diced
- 2 medium jalapeños peppers, seeded and minced
- ½ cup fresh cilantro, chopped
- ½ teaspoon salt
- 1 tablespoon fresh lime juice

White Sauce:
- ½ cup mayonnaise
- ½ cup plain low-fat Greek yogurt
- ⅓ cup fresh cilantro, chopped
- 2 tablespoons lime juice

Fried Shrimp Fritters
with Island Dressing
Serves 4 to 6

1. Fill Butterball® or Masterbuilt Fryer with oil. Heat to 375° F; this will take approximately 15 to 20 minutes.

2. Place the cooked shrimp, bell pepper, onions, and celery into a food processor and chop until very fine. In a large bowl, combine egg, milk, tomato paste, baking powder, flour, Tabasco sauce, and salt. Add shrimp mixture and combine all into a thick paste.

3. Using a tablespoon, drop shrimp mixture into oil, dividing fritters into 3 batches and cooking one batch at a time. Cook until golden brown, about 6 to 8 minutes. Serve hot as an appetizer, with island dressing.

Island Dressing:

1. In a medium-size bowl, combine mayonnaise, ketchup, egg, bell pepper, sweet relish, and hot sauce. Salt and pepper to taste. Serve with hot shrimp fritters for dipping.

Yields: 1 cup

You'll Need:

- 1 gallon cooking oil
- 1 lb. cocktail shrimp, pre-cooked
- ¾ red bell pepper, seeded and chopped
- ¾ cup onion, chopped
- ¼ cup celery, chopped
- 1 large egg
- 1 cup of milk
- 2 tablespoons tomato paste
- 1 teaspoon baking powder
- 1 ½ cups all purpose flour
- 1 teaspoon Tabasco sauce
- 1 teaspoon salt

Island Dressing:

- ½ cup mayonnaise
- 2 tablespoons ketchup or chili sauce
- 1 hard-boiled egg, mashed
- 2 tablespoons green bell pepper, chopped
- 1 tablespoon sweet relish
- 1 teaspoon hot sauce, your favorite brand
- Salt and black pepper

Deep-Fried Curried Fish Cakes

Serves 8 to 10

1. Fill Butterball® or Masterbuilt Fryer with oil. Heat to 375° F; this will take approximately 15 to 20 minutes.

2. In a large bowl, mix fish, potatoes, green onion, garlic, ginger, jalapeños, turmeric, coriander, curry powder, cilantro and salt. Place in refrigerator to chill.

3. Place the flour, eggs, and bread crumbs in three separate bowls. Form the fish mixture into balls about the size of a golf ball. Roll each ball in flour first, then in the egg to coat, and then in the bread crumbs.

4. Deep fry in oil for 6 minutes, until golden brown.

You'll Need:

- 1 gallon cooking oil
- 2 lbs. white fish (preferably Tilapia), finely chopped
- 1 lb. potatoes, cooked and mashed
- 1 bunch green onions, finely chopped
- 5 cloves garlic, minced
- 2 tablespoons fresh ginger, chopped
- 1 to 2 jalapeños peppers, finely chopped and seeds removed
- 1 teaspoon turmeric
- 1 teaspoon ground coriander
- 2 tablespoons curry powder
- ½ cup fresh cilantro, finely chopped
- 2 teaspoons salt
- 1 ½ cups flour
- 2 beaten eggs
- 1 ½ cups bread crumbs

JOHN *says*

Contrary to what many people think, curry is not a spice. Dozens of herbs and spices are combined to create what we call curry. If you want to give this dish a truly authentic flavor, serve it with a hot mango chutney or lime pickles on the side. These condiments are available in most grocery and Indian specialty stores.

Venetian-Style Fried Seafood and Vegetables

Serves 4

1. In a small bowl, combine the cornstarch and ⅓ cup of all-purpose, and ⅓ cup cake flour with sparkling water. Stir until it reaches the consistency of a thin batter. Season with salt and pepper to taste. Refrigerate batter for 2 hours. Chill shrimp, halibut and squid together in one bowl of ice water. Chill the scallops in a separate bowl of ice water.

2. Fill Butterball® or Masterbuilt Fryer with oil. Heat to 375° F; this will take approximately 15 to 20 minutes.

3. Drain shrimp, halibut and squid. Mix together remaining all-purpose and cake flour. Dredge seafood in flour mixture, and fry in batches until seafood is crisp, about 2 minutes per batch. Drain on paper towels and place in a warmed oven. Drain scallops, dredge in flour and fry separately until crisp, for 1 ½ minutes. Drain and place in the oven. Remove batter from the refrigerator, and dip beans, red pepper, and zucchini into batter to coat. Fry vegetables in batches until crisp, about 2 minutes. Drain on paper towels.

4. Remove seafood from oven, and toss lightly with vegetables on a platter. Sprinkle with a finishing salt and serve hot. May also be served with a marinara sauce for dipping.

You'll Need:
- ¼ cup corn starch
- 1 ½ cups all-purpose flour
- 1 ½ cups cake flour
- 1 cup sparkling water
- Salt and black pepper
- ¼ lb. peeled shrimp, whole
- ¼ lb. halibut, cut into 3-inch pieces
- ¼ lb. squid, cut into rings, with tentacle pieces
- ¼ lb. scallops
- 1 gallon cooking oil
- ¼ lb. green beans trimmed
- 1 medium red pepper, sliced into thin strips
- 1 medium zucchini, thinly sliced

Sesame Tempura Vegetables
with Soy Dipping Sauce
Serves 4

1. Fill Butterball® or Masterbuilt Fryer with oil. Heat to 375° F; this will take approximately 15 to 20 minutes.

2. To make batter, whisk together flour, sesame seeds, and sparkling water in a large bowl, until batter is smooth and has no lumps.

3. Toss about 10 vegetable pieces into batter and coat. Add vegetables to oil one at a time (to keep separate) and fry, turning them until golden, about 2 to 3 minutes. Transfer with tongs to paper towels to drain, and sprinkle with salt and pepper to taste. Coat and fry remaining vegetables in the same manner. Serve vegetables with dipping sauce.

Soy Dipping Sauce:

1. In a medium bowl combine oil, soy sauce, lime juice, and sugar, mixing well until sugar is dissolved.

You'll Need:
- 1 gallon cooking oil
- 2 cups all-purpose flour
- ½ cup (2 ounces) sesame seeds
- 2 cups sparkling water
- ½ lb. green beans, whole
- ½ lb. zucchini, sliced into 1-inch strips
- ½ lb. broccoli, florets
- 1 ½ lbs. parboiled sweet potatoes
- Salt and black pepper

Soy Dipping Sauce:
- 2 tablespoons vegetable oil
- 4 tablespoons soy sauce
- 4 teaspoons fresh squeezed lime juice
- 2 teaspoons sugar

JOHN *says*

Sometimes you only need to change one ingredient to turn a simple recipe into something really special. In this case, you might consider switching the flour with panko, Japanese-style bread crumbs. Panko looks like fluffy flakes of dried bread and adds an extra crispy crunch to tempura. The tempura batter will separate as you fry the vegetables. Skim this excess fried batter and serve as "cracklin."

Crab Hush Puppies
Honey-Mustard and Curry Sauce
Makes 30 hush puppies

1. Fill Butterball® or Masterbuilt Fryer with oil. Heat to 325° F; this will take approximately 15 to 20 minutes.

2. To make the dipping sauce, combine mustard, honey, and ¾ teaspoon curry powder in a small bowl.

3. In medium bowl, stir together cornbread mix, clam juice, and ½ teaspoon curry powder. Stir in crabmeat and ¾ cup green onions. Form this mixture into the shape and size of a golf-ball.

4. Working in batches of four, drop batter into fryer by tablespoon. Fry until golden and cooked through, for 1 to 1 ½ minutes. Use a metal slotted spoon to transfer to paper towels to drain. Sprinkle hush puppies with remaining green onions. Serve with dipping sauce.

You'll Need:
- 1 gallon cooking oil (preferably peanut oil)
- ¼ cup Creole mustard
- ¼ cup honey
- 1 ¼ teaspoons curry powder
- 1 (6 ounce) package instant cornbread mix (such as Martha White Buttermilk)
- ⅓ cup bottled clam juice
- 1 lb. fresh lump crabmeat, cleaned and drained
- 1 cup finely chopped green onions

JOHN *says*

This recipe is a fresh take on classic hush puppies. Pick your crabmeat over carefully to ensure that there aren't any shells. Remember to remove excess moisture from your crabmeat and check to make sure that your oil is 325° F. Oh, and did you know how the name "hush puppy" came about? Cooks used to fry up items in the kitchen and throw them outside to the dogs so they would "hush" during mealtime. My wife uses this same method on me... and it works! (Maybe we should call them "hush husbands.")

Deep-Fried Hot Dogs

Serves 4

1. Fill Butterball® or Masterbuilt Fryer with oil. Heat to 375° F; this will take approximately 15 to 20 minutes.

2. Place hot dogs into basket and lower into hot oil. Cook for 2 to 3 minutes. They will float to the top when done. For a crispier dog, cook for 1 to 2 more minutes.

3. Remove from oil and drain on paper towel. Place on bun and serve with all your favorite fixins.

You'll Need:
- 1 gallon cooking oil
- 1 (8-count) package hot dogs
- 1 (8-count) package hot dog buns
- 1 (8 ounce) jar relish (optional)

JOHN *says*

I am a Southerner with relatives in New Jersey that love to hear me talk. What they love even more is our version of one of their New Jersey favorites. These deep-fried hot dogs are a hit with both the kids and the grown-ups.

Deep-Fried Hamburgers
Serves 5

1. Fill Butterball® or Masterbuilt Fryer with oil. Heat to 375° F; this will take approximately 15 to 20 minutes.

2. In a medium bowl, combine ground chuck, onions, egg, garlic salt, and Worcestershire sauce.

3. Form meat mixture into 5 patties, each ¼-inch thick.

4. Fry until brown on each side.

You'll Need:
- 1 gallon cooking oil
- 1 lb. ground chuck
- ½ cup yellow onions, chopped
- 1 large egg
- ½ teaspoon garlic salt
- 2 teaspoons Worcestershire sauce

JOHN says

There is a restaurant in Memphis where you can sample what is believed to be the original deep-fried burger. The burgers are fried in grease that the management claims has not been changed since 1912. In fact, when the restaurant moved from its original location, the grease was transported with a police escort to a new, clean environment. Now, while we have full faith in the longevity of Masterbuilt fryers, we strongly recommend that you change your oil more than once every 100 years!

Fried Green Tomatoes

Serves 2 to 4

1. Fill Butterball® or Masterbuilt Fryer with oil. Heat to 375° F; this process will take approximately 15 to 20 minutes.

2. Wash tomatoes, and cut off the ends. Slice tomatoes ¼-inch thick and let the slices drain for 10 minutes, on paper towels. Season lightly with salt and pepper.

3. Pour milk into a shallow dish. In a resealable bag, combine cornmeal and flour. Place 4 to 6 tomato slices into the milk, then place slices into the bag, seal and shake to coat with cornmeal and flour mixture. Repeat this process until all tomato slices are coated. Place the prepared slices on a cutting board and scatter leftover cornmeal and flour over them. Cover slices with a paper towel.

4. Fry tomatoes for 1 ½ to 2 minutes. Drain on paper towels to remove excess oil. Plate to serve, and garnish with crumbled bacon bits and chopped parsley.

JOHN says

Long considered a staple in the South, this dish achieved notoriety in the movie "Fried Green Tomatoes." Slightly ripe and a little sour, they make a scrumptious side dish.

You'll Need:
- 1 gallon cooking oil
- 1 lb. medium green tomatoes (about 4)
- Pinch of salt
- Pinch of black pepper
- ⅓ cup milk
- ⅔ cup yellow cornmeal
- ½ cup all-purpose flour
- 4 slices bacon, cooked and finely crumbled
- 3 to 4 fresh parsley sprigs, finely chopped

Spicy Deep-Fried Oysters

Serves 4 to 6

1. Fill Butterball® or Masterbuilt Fryer with oil. Heat to 375° F; this will take approximately 15 to 20 minutes.

2. Rinse oysters and soak in fresh water for 20 minutes.

3. In a resealable plastic bag, combine the cornmeal, flour, garlic powder, Cajun seasoning, pepper, and seasoned salt. Place oysters in bag and shake until well-coated.

4. Cook oysters in small batches, 2 to 3 minutes per batch. Oysters will float and turn golden brown when done (internal temperature 145° F). Drain briefly and serve warm with your favorite cocktail sauce.

You'll Need:
- 1 gallon cooking oil
- 1 quart shucked oysters, drained
- 2 cups cornmeal
- 2 cups flour
- 4 tablespoons garlic powder
- 4 tablespoons Butterball® Cajun Seasoning
- 2 tablespoons black pepper
- 4 teaspoons seasoned salt

JOHN *says*

This recipe brings you within inches of an authentic Po' Boy sandwich. To go all the way, warm up a French baguette slice it horizontally and butter both sides. Pop the fried oysters on the bread, add lemon juice and ketchup, top them with dill pickles and you'll swear you're in Louisiana.

Crab Cakes
Quick Seafood Sauce

Makes 6 cakes

1. Fill Butterball® or Masterbuilt Fryer with oil. Heat to 375° F; this will take approximately 15 to 20 minutes.

2. Combine ⅓ cup bread crumbs, mayonnaise, eggs, mustard, green onion, Worcestershire sauce, and Butterball® Cajun Seasoning in large bowl and mix well. Add the crabmeat and mix well. With wet hands, form mixture into 6 cakes, each 3-inches wide. Set aside.

3. Place the remaining ⅔ cup bread crumbs into a shallow bowl. Dredge the crab cakes in crumbs and refrigerate uncovered for 1 hour.

4. Fry the crab cakes, turning once, about 1 ½ minutes or until golden brown. Remove from oil and transfer to paper towels to drain.

Sauce:

1. Mix mayonnaise, mustard, paprika, and hot sauce in a small bowl and serve over crab cakes or as a spicy dipping sauce.

JOHN *says*

A perfect crab cake is moist with a crisp crust and has enough spice to accent, not overpower, the taste of the crab. The cakes are wet when you form them but they get solid after an hour or so in the fridge. The starch in the bread makes a nice crust when the cakes are fried and the inside will be light and evenly seasoned.

You'll Need:
- 1 gallon cooking oil
- 1 cup dried bread crumbs
- ¼ cup mayonnaise
- 2 large eggs, beaten
- 1 tablespoon Dijon mustard
- 1 green onion, finely chopped
- ½ teaspoon Worcestershire sauce
- ½ teaspoon Butterball Cajun Seasoning
- 1 lb. fresh lump crabmeat, cleaned and drained well

Sauce:
- ¼ cup mayonnaise
- 1 tablespoon mustard
- ¼ teaspoon paprika
- ¼ teaspoon hot sauce

Chicken Fried Steaks

Serves 8

1. Fill Butterball® or Masterbuilt Fryer with oil. Heat to 375° F; this will take approximately 15 to 20 minutes.

2. In a medium bowl, whisk together the eggs and milk. In a separate bowl, combine the flour and beef seasoning.

3. Dip the first 4 cutlets into the egg mixture, one at a time. Dredge them in the flour, then dip them back into the egg mixture, and very gently place them in the hot oil. Cook 1 minute per side, depending on the thickness of meat. Fry until the breading is a golden brown color. Carefully remove the basket from the fryer and drain cutlets on a platter lined with paper towels. Repeat the process for the remaining 4 cutlets.

You'll Need:

- 1 gallon cooking oil
- 2 eggs
- 2 cups milk, room temperature
- 3 cups flour
- 2 teaspoons beef seasoning
- 8 (6 ounce) beef cutlets, tenderized at room temperature

JOHN *says*

This dish is the Granddaddy of all Southern comfort food. If you're not from the South, you should know it's not chicken, and no, it doesn't taste like chicken. It tastes like steak, fried like chicken.

Pecan Catfish
Pepper Pecan Sauce
Serves 6

1. Fill Butterball® or Masterbuilt Fryer with oil. Heat to 375° F; this will take approximately 15 to 20 minutes.

2. Preheat oven to 400° F. Spread all the pecans on a baking sheet and toast for 8 minutes, stirring occasionally, until lightly browned and aromatic. Transfer pecans to a plate and let cool.

3. In a food processor, pulse 1 cup of the cooled pecans just until they resemble coarse meal, saving remainder of pecans for garnishing. Do not over-process.

4. Rinse the fish filets and pat dry with paper towels. In a shallow bowl, whisk together the buttermilk and eggs. In another shallow bowl, stir together the flour, cornmeal, ¾ cup pecan meal, salt, and pepper. Dip each filet into the buttermilk mixture, then coat evenly with the flour mixture, shaking off any excess. Place coated filets onto a baking sheet.

5. Working in batches, fry the filets until golden brown on the outside and meat is opaque on the inside, about 5 minutes. Using a metal spatula, carefully remove filets from basket and transfer to paper towels to drain. Keep warm until all the filets are cooked. Garnish with lemon wedges and pecan halves. Pass around the chilled sauce at the table.

You'll Need:
- 1 gallon cooking oil
- 1 ½ cups pecans halves
- 6 (6 ounce) catfish filets
- 1 cup buttermilk
- 2 large eggs
- ½ cup unbleached all-purpose flour
- 1 cup yellow cornmeal
- ¼ teaspoon salt
- ¼ teaspoon black pepper
- Lemon wedges for garnish

Pepper Pecan Sauce:
- 1 cup mayonnaise
- 1 shallot, finely chopped
- 1 jalapeño chili, seeded and finely chopped
- 2 tablespoons sweet pickle relish
- 2 tablespoons fresh dill, chopped
- Juice of 1 medium lemon
- ¼ teaspoon salt
- ¼ teaspoon black pepper

Pepper Pecan Sauce:

1. In food processor, combine ¼ cup pecan meal, mayonnaise, shallots, jalapeños, pickle relish, dill, lemon juice, salt and pepper. Pulse until well blended but still chunky. Transfer to a serving bowl, cover, and refrigerate until ready to serve.

Sweet and Sour Chicken

Serves 6-8

1. Fill Butterball® or Masterbuilt Fryer with oil. Heat to 375° F; this will take approximately 15 to 20 minutes.

2. Sprinkle 1 teaspoon salt evenly over chicken pieces. In a large bowl, combine remaining salt, flour, cornstarch, and baking powder. In a small bowl, combine milk and eggs. Add milk mixture to flour mixture and stir until batter is smooth.

3. Dip chicken pieces in batter and fry for 5 minutes. Drain on paper towels to remove excess oil.

Sauce:

1. Heat peanut oil in a large sauté pan over medium-high heat. Add onion and bell pepper pieces and sauté for 3 minutes.

2. Add ginger and garlic and sauté for 1 minute more. Add vinegar, sugar, soy sauce, and pineapple chunks and cook 2 minutes more, stirring constantly.

3. In a small bowl, combine reserved pineapple juice, cornstarch, and food coloring. Stir until smooth.

4. Add juice mixture to the pan and bring to a boil. Cook 1 minute, stirring constantly. Remove from heat and serve with chicken and rice.

JOHN says

We believe that everything tastes better when cooked at home, so if you've got a taste for Chinese food, skip the take-out menu and serve this quick and simple dish. It also works well with any mild fish.

You'll Need:

- 1 gallon cooking oil
- 4 (6 ounce) boneless, skinless chicken breasts, cut into bite-sized pieces
- 1 ½ teaspoons salt
- 1 cup all-purpose flour
- ½ cup cornstarch
- ½ teaspoon baking powder
- 1 cup milk
- 2 large eggs, beaten
- Cooked rice, enough for 8 people

Sauce:
- 4 tablespoons peanut oil
- 2 cups yellow onion, cut into 1-inch pieces
- 2 green bell peppers, cut into 1-inch pieces
- 3 teaspoons fresh ginger, grated
- 2 cloves garlic, minced
- ⅔ cup distilled white vinegar
- 6 tablespoons sugar
- 4 tablespoons soy sauce
- 2 (20 ounce) cans pineapple chunks, drained and juice reserved
- 4 tablespoons cornstarch
- 1 drop red food coloring

Shrimp Tempura

Serves 4

1. Fill Butterball® or Masterbuilt Fryer oil. Heat to 375 F; this will take approximately 15 to 20 minutes.

2. Combine flour and salt in medium mixing bowl. Stir in cold water and egg yolk, mixing just enough to combine. In another bowl, beat the egg white until frothy and fold into the batter. Mixture should be thin.

3. Dip shrimp in batter (hold it by the tail so as not to coat) and then cover battered shrimp, except for the tail, in panko. Fry until golden brown, about 3 to 5 minutes on each side, turning as needed for even browning. Drain on paper towels.

4. Serve immediately with sauce.

Ginger, Mango, and Lime Sauce:

1. In a small saucepan, mix ginger, soy sauce, mango, lime juice, red chili, shallots, and brown sugar and bring to a boil. Cool and puree in a blender. Serve with shrimp for dipping.

You'll Need:

- 1 gallon cooking oil (preferably peanut oil)
- 1 cup all-purpose flour
- ¼ teaspoon salt
- 1 to 1 ¼ cups of cold water
- 1 egg, separated
- 1 lb. medium shrimp, cleaned
- ½ cup panko (Japanese-style breadcrumbs)

Ginger, Mango, and Lime Sauce:

- 2 tablespoons fresh ginger, minced
- 2 tablespoons soy sauce
- 1 fresh mango, peeled and diced
- Juice of 2 limes
- 1 small red chili minced, or ½ teaspoon cayenne pepper
- 1 shallot, minced
- 1 tablespoon light brown sugar

JOHN says

Always remember to individually add the shrimp to the fryer, separating them with a metal spatula while frying. Don't overcrowd. I typically fry 8 to 10 shrimp at a time. This recipe goes nicely with tempura vegetables. (See recipe, page 45.) If you like a little kick with your shrimp, sprinkle some Butterball® Cajun Seasoning onto them before applying the batter.

Fried Wings

Serves 3 to 5

1. Fill Butterball® or Masterbuilt Fryer with oil to the MAX line. Heat to 375° F; this will take approximately 15 to 20 minutes.

2. Place wings in a large bowl. Pour soy sauce over wings, cover and chill in refrigerator for 1 hour. Drain and pat dry with paper towels.

3. Place wings into the fryer basket and carefully lower into the fryer; cook for 10 to 12 minutes, turning occasionally. Be careful not to overcrowd or stack wings in the basket. Using a metal spatula or slotted spoon, remove wings from fryer and place in a single layer on paper towels.

4. In a small bowl, combine pepper, garlic powder, and cayenne pepper. Sprinkle mixture over wings, turning to coat both sides.

You'll Need:
- 1 gallon cooking oil
- 2 lbs. chicken wings
- 1 cup soy sauce
- 1 tablespoon black pepper
- 1 teaspoon garlic powder
- ¼ teaspoon cayenne pepper

JOHN says

It is best to season wings while they're hot, right out of the oil. For even simpler preparation of this recipe, substitute the spices in Step 4 with Butterball® Cajun Seasoning. Don't forget to serve with a bowl of ranch or bleu cheese dressing, along with celery and carrot sticks!

Cornish Game Hens

Serves 8

1. Fill Butterball® Indoor Electric Turkey Fryer with oil to the MAX line. Heat to 375° F; this will take approximately 15 to 20 minutes.

2. Completely thaw Cornish game hens, if frozen. Rinse game hens thoroughly with warm water or soak in a warm water bath for no more than 15 minutes to ensure that cavities are free of ice. Pat game hens completely dry on outside and inside of cavities with paper towels.

3. Using a injector syringe, inject ¼ cup (2 ounces) marinade into each game hen. Sprinkle hen generously with Cajun Turkey Seasoning, outside and inside.

4. Place game hen(s) breast side up in basket or on Masterbuilt's accessory rack. Slowly lower basket or rack into hot oil; be cautious of splattering oil. Fry 1 to 4 game hen(s) for a total of 14 to 15 minutes or until internal temperature reaches 165° F in the breast (use an oven thermometer to test temperature, but make sure that you remove the hen from the hot oil to test). Slowly lift the basket or rack from the hot oil, hooking the drain clip on basket into drain clip mounting hole.

5. Once game hens reach desired temperature, turn the fryer to MIN and unplug from the outlet. Allow game hens to rest in fryer basket and drain for 5 minutes before removing. Place on paper towels to rest for 10 minutes. Carve and serve.

You'll Need:
- 2 gallons cooking oil
- 4 Cornish game hens, fresh or frozen
- 1 (16 ounce) bottle Butterball® Buttery Creole Turkey Marinade
- Butterball® Cajun Turkey seasoning for coating

JOHN *says*

Don and I are known for deep-frying turkeys, which ALWAYS get rave reviews. We find that those same raves come with this recipe. You will get tender, juicy results everytime! Cut'em in half and you can serve two people per bird.

Fried Scotch Eggs

Serves 4

You'll Need:

- 1 gallon cooking oil
- 1 ¼ lbs. breakfast sausage
- 2 green onions, finely chopped
- 2 tablespoons fresh rosemary, finely chopped
- 1 teaspoon salt
- ½ teaspoon black pepper
- 2 tablespoons all-purpose flour
- 1 cup dry bread crumbs
- 1 large egg, beaten
- 4 hard boiled eggs, shelled

1. Fill Butterball® or Masterbuilt Fryer with oil. Heat to 375° F; this will take approximately 15 to 20 minutes.

2. In a medium bowl, combine the sausage, onions, rosemary, salt, and pepper. Divide this mixture into four equal parts. Place the flour, bread crumbs and beaten egg into three separate bowls. Take a hard-boiled egg and dredge it in the flour mixture. Then form one sausage section around the egg, patting it into a baseball-sized shape. Roll the ball into the beaten egg and then dredge it in the bread crumbs. Repeat this process for the three remaining eggs and sausage.

3. Deep fry for 10 to 12 minutes, until pork is cooked. Cool and cut each Scotch Egg in half to serve.

JOHN *says*

I must admit, this is not a recipe my momma made, but I love being creative and will try anything. We brought Scotch eggs to our Southern kitchen and both Momma and I think it is pretty *Dadgum Good!*

Spicy Fried Calamari
with Lemon Dipping Sauce
Serves 4

1. Fill Butterball® or Masterbuilt Fryer with oil. Heat to 375° F; this will take approximately 15 to 20 minutes.

2. In a large bowl, pour buttermilk over calamari. Stir in 1 tablespoon Cajun seasoning and let marinate for about 5 minutes.

3. In another large bowl, combine cornmeal, flour, and remaining 3 tablespoons of Cajun seasoning. Add the calamari and turn until all the pieces are thoroughly coated.

4. Fry the calamari for 1 or 2 minutes until light golden brown. Using a metal, slotted spoon, transfer to paper towel to drain. Serve immediately with lemon wedges and lemon dipping sauce.

Sauce:
1. In a medium bowl mix dill, Cajun seasoning, pepper, zest of lemon, lemon juice, and mayonnaise. Refrigerate until ready to serve.

You'll Need:
- 1 gallon cooking oil
- 3 lbs. frozen calamari, thawed and patted dry
- 2 cups buttermilk
- 4 tablespoons Butterball® Cajun Seasoning
- 1 ½ cups cornmeal
- 2 cups all-purpose flour
- Lemon wedges

Sauce:
- 1 tablespoon fresh dill, chopped
- 2 teaspoons Butterball Cajun Seasoning
- 1 teaspoon black pepper
- 2 lemons, juiced and peels reserved for zest
- 1 cup mayonnaise

JOHN *says*

While frying the calamari or any other small seafoods or pieces of meat, make sure you drop them in separately and don't let them clump together. Use a metal ladle to keep them separated while frying.

Twice Fried Fries

Serves 4

1. Fill Butterball® or Masterbuilt Fryer with oil. Heat to 375° F; this will take approximately 15 to 20 minutes.

2. Peel and cut potatoes into ¼- inch thick strips.

3. Fry potatoes 2 to 3 minutes until they just begin to soften. Remove potatoes from oil and place on a cookie sheet lined with paper towels, spreading the potatoes out allowing them to drain thoroughly. Fry potatoes an additional 3 to 4 minutes until golden brown. Remove and drain on paper towels.

4. In a small bowl, combine salt, black pepper, white pepper, and garlic powder. While potatoes are still hot, sprinkle seasoning mixture over them.

You'll Need:
- 1 gallon cooking oil
- 2 to 3 lbs. Russet potatoes
- 1 tablespoon salt
- 1 tablespoon black pepper
- 2 teaspoons white pepper
- 2 teaspoons garlic powder

JOHN *says*

Two reasons why these fries taste so good: (1.) They're cooked twice. (2.) They're fried in a Masterbuilt Fryer, which always maintains an even cooking temperature. So even though the fries are cooled before you cook them again, they fry evenly and come out crunchy on the outside and light and fluffy on the inside. For a special treat, serve with sea salt.

Deep-Fried Oreos

Serves 4 to 6

1. Fill Butterball® or Masterbuilt Fryer with oil. Heat to 375° F; this will take approximately 15 to 20 minutes.

2. In a medium bowl, whisk together the egg, milk, and vegetable oil. Stir in the pancake mix until no dry lumps remain. Dip the cookies into the batter one at a time, and carefully place into the hot oil, frying only 4 or 5 at a time to avoid overcrowding.

3. Fry the cookies 1 minute per side, until they are golden-brown. Drain on a paper towel. Sprinkle with confectioners' sugar and serve warm.

You'll Need:

- 1 gallon cooking oil
- 1 large egg
- 1 cup milk
- 2 teaspoons vegetable oil
- 1 ½ cups pancake mix
- 1 (18 ounce) package Oreo cookies
- ½ cup confectioners' sugar

JOHN *says*

Just when you think dessert can't get any more decadent, along comes the deep-fried Oreo. Question is, does it count as a dessert or a side dish? Sitting there all golden and puffy on the side of your plate, it could pass as a pumpkin fritter. But one bite will tell you it's definitely not a member of any recommended food group. Go ahead, indulge yourself.

Pumpkin Fritters

Serves 6 to 8

1. Fill Butterball® or Masterbuilt Fryer with oil. Heat to 375° F; this will take approximately 15 to 20 minutes.

2. In a medium bowl, combine the pumpkin, egg, flour, baking powder, cinnamon, and mace, mix well.

3. Drop 1 tablespoon of batter at a time into fryer. Fry for 5 to 6 minutes until fritters turn golden brown.

4. Drain well on paper towels. Sprinkle fritters with cinnamon sugar and serve warm with syrup.

Syrup:

1. In a small saucepan, combine the sugar, water, and cornflour. Bring to a slow boil, stirring constantly until the sugar dissolves. Continue to boil until the mixture becomes syrupy enough to coat the back of a spoon.

2. Pour syrup into a gravy boat or a sauce bowl and serve with fritters.

You'll Need:
- 1 gallon cooking oil
- 2 cups canned pumpkin
- 1 egg, lightly beaten
- 2 cups cake flour
- 1 ½ teaspoons baking powder
- ¼ teaspoon cinnamon
- ¼ teaspoon mace
- Cinnamon sugar for sprinkling

Syrup:
- ½ cup dark brown sugar
- ½ cup water
- 1 teaspoon corn flour

JOHN *says*

These work great with either canned or fresh pumpkin. They make a great side dish for a holiday dinner and you can change up the flavor by adding ginger, nutmeg, or allspice. If you are running short on time, use your favorite store-bought syrup.

Mini Fried Pecan Pies

Serves 4 to 8

1. Fill Butterball® or Masterbuilt Fryer with oil. Heat to 375° F; this will take approximately 15 to 20 minutes.

2. While oil heats, cream the butter and sugar with an electric mixer. Beat in syrup, flour, salt, and vanilla extract. Stir in pecans until well-mixed.

3. Unroll pie crusts and cut into 16 circles using a 4-inch cookie cutter (or a glass mug that is wide enough). This requires re-rolling twice using the leftover of crust. Spoon 1 tablespoon filling in the center of each crust circle. Fold dough in half, creating a half-moon shape. Seal and crimp the open edges using the tines of a fork.

4. Fry the pies in batches of two at 350° F for 3 minutes until golden brown, turning occasionally to brown evenly. Remove pies and place on paper towels to drain. Let cool slightly and dust with confectioners' sugar if desired.

You'll Need:

- 1 gallon cooking oil
- ⅓ cup butter, softened
- ½ cup sugar
- ¼ cup Golden Eagle syrup
- 1 tablespoon self-rising flour
- ¼ teaspoon salt
- 1 teaspoon vanilla extract
- 1 cup chopped pecans
- 1 (15 ounce) package refrigerated pie crusts
- Confectioners' sugar (optional)

JOHN says

When I heard that Maryland Tracy of Calera, Alabama, bakes a pecan pie that makes people slap themselves, I had to taste it. One bite and I was sold. Maryland suggested that we take her recipe and pop them in the fryer. Well, we did and served these little guys with a scoop of vanilla ice cream. It made us slap ourselves twice!

Deep-Fried Mars Bars

Serves 4

1. Chill the chocolate bars in the refrigerator, (not the freezer), for 3 hours.

2. Fill Butterball® or Masterbuilt Fryer with oil. Heat to 375° F; this will take approximately 15 to 20 minutes.

3. In a medium bowl, combine the plain flour, cornflour, and baking soda. Continue to stir and add mineral water until you get a batter with the consistency of thin cream.

4. Remove Mars Bars from wrappers. Coat completely with the batter. Using the fryer basket, carefully lower bars into hot oil and fry until golden brown. Remove from fryer and divide between 4 plates. Serve with ice cream.

You'll Need:
- 2 Mars Bars, or your favorite candy bar
- 1 gallon cooking oil
- 1 cup plain flour
- ½ cup corn flour
- 1/16 teaspoon baking soda
- Mineral water

JOHN *says*

A crunchy exterior gives way to a flood of delicious molten chocolate. This is a treat that's taken the world by storm and what is usually added to menus as just a gimmick, fast becomes a permanent fixture. It's time to take your chocolate cravings to a whole new level!

Fried Banana Fritters

Serves 4

1. Fill Butterball® or Masterbuilt Fryer with oil. Heat to 375° F; this will take approximately 15 to 20 minutes.

2. Combine the cake flour, coconut flour, flaked coconut, coconut milk, salt, sugar, and sesame seeds in a large bowl, and mix until the batter is smooth. Cut the bananas into 3 equal sections then cut each section into 1-inch strips.

3. Dip the banana pieces in the batter, shaking off any excess batter before you place pieces in the oil. Fry in small batches for 2 to 3 minutes until golden brown. Remove banana fritters from fryer and place on paper towels to drain. Sprinkle with confectioners' sugar. Serve immediately.

You'll Need:

- 1 gallon cooking oil
- 1 cup cake flour
- 1 cup coconut flour
- ¼ cup flaked coconut
- 1 cup coconut milk
- ½ teaspoon salt
- ¼ cup granulated sugar
- 1 teaspoon sesame seeds
- 3 large unripened bananas (skins still green, or just turning yellow)
- ¼ cup confectioners' sugar

JOHN *says*

Serve up these as appetizers and complement them with a sweet and spicy dipping sauce or as a dessert with ice cream and hot chocolate sauce. WOW!

Fried Ice Cream

Serves 4 to 6

1. Use ice cream scoop and dip out several level scoops. Place on large tray, cover with waxed paper, and place in freezer for at least 2 hours.

2. Combine water and eggs in a large bowl to make an egg wash. Place corn flakes, cinnamon, and sugar in a plastic resealable bag, and crush corn flakes until no large pieces remain. Place corn flake mixture in a medium-size bowl. Working quickly, remove ice cream balls from freezer and place in corn flake mixture. Coat completely, pressing corn flakes into ice cream ball. Roll ice cream ball in egg wash and coat completely. Finally, return the ice cream ball to the corn flake mixture and coat completely, pressing corn flakes into ball lightly. Place on large tray, cover, and return to freezer for 2 hours.

3. Fill Butterball® or Masterbuilt Fryer with oil. Heat to 375° F; this will take approximately 15 to 20 minutes. When oil has reached 375° F, remove ice cream balls from freezer. Working quickly drop ice cream balls one at a time into oil, and cook for approximately 15 seconds, until golden brown. Remove and drain quickly on paper towels. Return fried ice cream ball to the freezer as you continue to fry additional balls.

4. Remove from freezer and serve with your favorite toppings or freeze for later.

You'll Need:

- ½ gallon ice cream (preferably Blue Bell)
- 2 ounces (¼ cup) water
- 2 eggs
- 3 cups corn flakes or frosted corn flakes cereal
- 2 tablespoons cinnamon
- 3 tablespoons sugar
- 1 gallon cooking oil

Suggested Garnishes:

- Honey
- Whipped cream
- Chocolate syrup
- Confectioners' sugar

JOHN says

If you think the idea of frying ice cream is over the top, consider warming and melting a Mars Bar in a saucepan and drizzle it on the fried ice cream. Now that's over the top!

Yeast Doughnuts

Serves 8 to 10

1. Fill Butterball® or Masterbuilt Fryer with oil. Heat to 350° F; this will take approximately 15 to 20 minutes.

2. Heat milk in small saucepan over medium heat, until milk begins to bubble at the edges. Place shortening in a small bowl. Pour milk over shortening and stir with a whisk. Set aside and let cool to lukewarm.

3. In a small bowl, sprinkle the yeast over warm water (approximately 100° F). Let stand for 5 minutes. Pour yeast mixture into a large bowl. Add shortening mixture, eggs, sugar, salt, nutmeg, and 3 cups of flour which has been spooned into a measuring cup and leveled with a knife. Stir well with a wooden spoon until mixture is well combined. Gradually add the remaining flour and stir again. Dough will be sticky, but should begin to come together. Resist the urge to add more flour. Using your floured hands, knead the dough in bowl for 3 to 4 minutes, or until dough is smooth and forms a ball.

4. Place dough in well-greased bowl, turning to coat top. Cover and place in a draft-free area for 45 minutes or until dough rises to twice its size.

5. On a well-floured surface, roll out dough to ½-inch thickness. Using a 3-inch pastry ring, cut out circles, and use a 1-inch ring to cut out center hole in each circle. Place doughnuts on a floured surface and cover with plastic wrap. Let dough rest 15 minutes.

6. Cook doughnuts 3 or 4 minutes each, 45 to 60 seconds per side, or until golden brown.

7. Place doughnuts on a cooling rack, set over a lined baking sheet for 10 minutes. Glaze doughnuts when cool, collecting and reusing the glaze that passes through rack and onto baking sheet.

Makes about 20 doughnuts.

You'll Need:

- 1 gallon cooking oil
- 1 ½ cups whole milk
- ⅓ cup vegetable shortening
- 2 packages active dry yeast
- ⅓ cup warm water
- 2 large eggs, lightly beaten
- ¼ cup sugar
- 1 teaspoon salt
- ¼ teaspoon ground nutmeg
- 6 cups unbleached all-purpose flour

Glaze:
- ½ stick (¼ cup) butter, melted
- ¼ cup warm milk
- 3 cups confectioners' sugar
- ½ teaspoon salt
- ½ teaspoon vanilla

Glaze:

1. In a medium saucepan, melt butter, then add the milk, confectioners' sugar, salt, and vanilla. Mix until smooth about 5 minutes. Brush or spoon warm glaze over doughnuts.

Beignets
Serves 10 to 12

1. In a large bowl, whisk together warm water, sugar, and yeast; let stand 10 minutes.

2. In another large bowl, whisk together eggs, salt, and evaporated milk. Add egg mixture to yeast mixture, stirring with a whisk. Add 3 cups flour and shortening, stirring with a wooden spoon to combine.

3. Add remaining flour, ½ cup at a time. Remove dough from bowl and place on a lightly floured surface. Knead 3 to 4 minutes or until smooth.

4. Place dough in a slightly oiled large bowl, cover with a towel, and place in warm place to rise for 1 hour and 45 minutes, or until dough is almost doubled in bulk.

5. Fill Butterball® or Masterbuilt Fryer with oil. Preheat to 350° F; this will take approximately 15 to 20 minutes. While oil is heating, place dough on floured surface and roll out to approximately ¼-inch thickness. With sharp knife, cut into 2-inch squares. Place 4 squares at a time in basket and fry in oil. (Keep cut dough covered with a towel while frying.) Do not stack the dough squares in the basket. Dough should float to top while cooking. Turn beignets frequently, cooking until golden brown – approximately 3 to 4 minutes.

6. Drain beignets on cake rack over cookie sheet or jelly roll pan. Dust with confectioners' sugar and serve warm.

Makes about 50

You'll Need:
- 1 ½ cups warm water (105° F to 110° F)
- ¾ cup sugar
- 1 (¼ ounce) envelope active dry yeast
- 3 large eggs
- 1 teaspoon salt
- 1 cup evaporated milk
- 6 ½ to 7 cups unbleached bread flour
- ¼ cup shortening
- 1 gallon cooking oil
- Confectioners' sugar, for dusting

JOHN *says*

You don't have to be at a café in New Orleans to enjoy these piping hot beignets. This recipe brings the sweetness to your own kitchen. To keep your beignets from sticking to the basket, I suggest you leave the basket in the fryer while the oil is preheating, to keep it hot, then use a ladle to carefully lower the dough squares into the fryer. Once they are golden brown, lift the basket to drain.

Marinated Steamed Shrimp

Serves 8 to 10

1. Fill Butterball® or Masterbuilt Fryer to the MAX fill line with water. Set to 375° F and bring to a boil. This will take approximately 15 to 20 minutes. Although cooking time on this recipe is short, water may need to be added if steamer is used for more than 60 minutes.

2. Place shrimp in the steamer basket, close lid and steam 4 to 5 minutes, or until shrimp turns pink, stirring occasionally. (Note: Do not lower basket into water when steaming.) Remove steamer basket, drain the shrimp, and rinse with cold water. Place shrimp in a large bowl and chill for 1 hour in the refrigerator.

3. In a shallow dish, combine the sugar, vinegar, oil, capers, salt, and celery salt. Add the shrimp and onions and mix. Cover and chill for at least 6 hours, turning the mixture often.

You'll Need:
- 2 lbs. medium shrimp, peeled and deveined
- ½ cup sugar
- 1 ¼ cups white balsamic vinegar
- 1 cup vegetable oil
- ¼ cup capers, drained
- 1 teaspoon salt
- 1 ½ teaspoons celery salt
- 1 medium red onion, thinly sliced

JOHN *says*

To devein or not to devein? That is the question when it comes to preparing fresh shrimp. It's not necessary to remove the "sand vein." Many cooks do so for aesthetic reasons, and the vein can give your shrimp a gritty texture. The vein in small shrimp is so tiny, it virtually disappears during cooking, but you may want to remove the vein when cooking medium to large shrimp.

Steamed Vegetables
Serves 6 to 8

1. Fill Butterball® or Masterbuilt Fryer to the MAX fill line with water. Set to 375° F and bring to a boil; this will take approximately 15 to 20 minutes. Although cooking time on this recipe is short, water may need to be added if steamer is used for more than 60 minutes.

2. In the steamer basket, layer sliced red potatoes first, then carrots, then squash, and finally the onion. Lightly sprinkle each layer with sea salt and pepper.

3. Cover and steam at 375° F, until the potatoes are done and the carrots are tender but still crisp, approximately 6 to 8 minutes. (Note: Do not lower basket into water when steaming.)

4. Remove vegetables from steamer and place into a large serving bowl; toss with the extra virgin olive oil to coat, and serve warm.

You'll Need:
- 2 lbs. red potatoes, unpeeled, cut into ¼-inch thick slices
- 6 carrots, sliced ¼-inch thick
- 2 lbs. squash, cubed
- 2 large onions, sliced ¼-inch thick
- ¹⁄₁₆ teaspoon sea salt
- ¹⁄₁₆ teaspoon black pepper
- 2 tablespoons extra virgin olive oil

JOHN *says*

The reason I love to steam vegetables instead of boiling them is because steaming does not boil the nutrients or the flavor away . Plus, it's *Dadgum* easy!

Sweet and Spicy Asian Style Meatballs

Serves 2 to 4

1. Fill Butterball® or Masterbuilt Fryer to the MAX fill line with water. Set to 375° F and bring to a boil. This will take approximately 15 to 20 minutes. Although cooking time on this recipe is short, water may need to be added if steamer is used for more than 60 minutes.

2. Place the beef in a food processor, pulse and slowly add egg white and cold water, blending well. Place beef mixture in medium-size bowl. Add salt, soy sauce, pepper, sesame oil, cilantro, onions, flour, sugar, and chili flakes and mix until it is a light paste. Using your hands, form the mixture into 1 ½-inch meatballs, about the size of a golf ball.

3. Place the meatballs in the steamer basket and use the drain clip to hook basket on inner pot. (Note: Do not lower basket into water when steaming.) Cover with lid and steam for 20 minutes, or until internal temperature reaches 160° F. Remove meatballs from steamer basket, and turn onto a serving plate or bowl. Sprinkle with chili flakes and serve.

JOHN *says*

The secret to achieving a light texture in these meatballs lies in the egg white and flour. You can make these ahead of time and steam them lightly just before your guests arrive. They make a great appetizer.

You'll Need:
- 1 lb. ground sirloin
- 1 egg white
- 1 tablespoon ice cold water
- ½ teaspoon salt
- 1 tablespoon soy sauce
- 1 teaspoon black pepper
- 2 teaspoons sesame oil
- 1 tablespoon cilantro, finely chopped
- 2 green onions, chopped
- 1 teaspoon all-purpose flour
- 1 teaspoon sugar
- 1 tablespoon chili flakes

Greek Chicken Packets

Serves 4

1. Fill Butterball® or Masterbuilt Fryer to the MAX fill line with water. Set to 375° F and bring to a boil. This will take approximately 15 to 20 minutes. Although cooking time on this recipe is short, water may need to be added if steamer is used for more than 60 minutes.

2. Using aluminum foil, cut 4 (15-inch) squares; fold in half to make a crease and open up. Place chicken over the seam in center of foils. Sprinkle evenly with Greek seasoning, salt, and pepper. Top with artichokes, tomatoes, and olives. Drizzle evenly with olive oil and lemon juice. Place a sprig of oregano on top of each piece of chicken. Fold aluminum foil over the chicken mixture to create an air-tight packet.

3. Place packets in steamer basket, and hook basket with drain clip on inner pot. (Note: Do not lower basket into water when steaming.) Cover and steam 30 to 35 minutes, or until chicken is tender. Carefully open packets and sprinkle with feta cheese, then reseal until it is time to serve.

You'll Need:
- 4 (6 to 8 ounces) boneless skinless chicken breasts, halved
- 1 teaspoon Greek seasoning
- ½ teaspoon salt
- ½ teaspoon black pepper
- 1 (14 ounce) can quartered artichokes, drained
- 1 pint grape tomatoes, halved
- ⅓ cup pitted kalamata olives, halved
- 2 tablespoons extra virgin olive oil
- 2 tablespoons lemon juice
- 4 small sprigs fresh oregano
- ¼ cup crumbled feta cheese

STEAMED

JOHN says

Cooking in foil is a classic technique for preparing delicious and healthy meals. Slice your vegetables thinly and evenly to ensure that vegetables cook thoroughly. Also, be sure to seal the edges of foil packet completely to prevent steam from escaping while the food cooks. If you're serving this dish at a dinner party, place a pouch on each plate and let your guests enjoy the aroma that floats up as they carefully open the foil packets.

Pork Dumplings
with Sweet Soy Dipping Sauce

Serves 4 to 6

1. Combine garlic, ginger, green onions and red bell pepper in a food processor; pulse until minced. Add pork, soy sauce, and sesame oil. Pulse until mixture is well combined.

2. Drop mixture by heaping teaspoonfuls onto centers of wonton wrappers. Brush edges of wrappers with water. Gather corners of wrapper together to form an "x" crimping sides to seal. Repeat process with remaining wrappers, covering dumplings with damp paper towels as you make them so they don't dry out. Makes approximately 24 dumplings.

3. Meanwhile, fill Butterball® or Masterbuilt Fryer to the MAX fill line with water. Set to 375° F and bring to a boil. This will take approximately 15 to 20 minutes. Although cooking time on this recipe is short, water may need to be added if steamer is used for more than 60 minutes. Line the steamer basket with cabbage leaves. Place half of wontons in one layer in basket. Cover and steam 8 to 10 minutes. (Note: Do not lower basket into water when steaming.) Repeat with second batch. Serve warm with Sweet Soy Dipping Sauce.

You'll Need:

- 2 cloves garlic
- 1 (2-inch) piece fresh ginger root, peeled
- 2 green onions, quartered
- ½ cup red bell pepper, cubed
- ½ lb. ground pork
- 1 tablespoon soy sauce
- 2 teaspoons dark sesame oil
- 32 wonton wrappers
- 4 to 6 cabbage leaves

Sweet Soy Dipping Sauce:
- 2 tablespoons ginger root, peeled and minced
- ⅔ cup soy sauce
- 2 tablespoons dark sesame oil
- ¼ cup rice vinegar
- ¼ cup firmly packed brown sugar
- ¼ to ½ teaspoon crushed red pepper

Sweet Soy Dipping Sauce:

1. In a small bowl, combine all sauce ingredients. Makes about 1 cup.

JOHN *says*

If you can't find ground pork at your supermarket, you can use chicken, turkey or beef in this recipe. The Sweet Dipping Sauce gets its nutty, toasted flavor from sesame oil, which is renowned for its medicinal qualities. So, eat up and stay healthy!

Sweet Corn
with Cilantro Chili Butter
Serves 4

1. Fill Butterball® or Masterbuilt Fryer to the MAX fill line with water. Set to 375° F and bring to a boil. This will take approximately 15 to 20 minutes. Although cooking time on this recipe is short, water may need to be added if steamer is used for more than 60 minutes. Using the drain clip, hook the basket on the inner pot.

2. Husk corn and rinse.

3. Coat the steamer basket with nonstick cooking spray or line with a layer of corn husks. (Note: Do not lower basket into water when steaming.) Cover and steam the corn for 30 minutes.

Cilantro Chili Butter:

1. Mix butter, jalapeño, cilantro, cayenne, lime zest, lime juice, onion powder, and garlic in a medium bowl. Place butter mixture on rectangular piece of wax paper, roll into a cylinder and freeze.

2. To serve, slice the butter into 2-inch medallions. Place a medallion of butter on each piece of steamed corn.

You'll Need:
- 4 ears of corn, husked

Cilantro Chili Butter:
- 1 cup (2 sticks) butter, softened
- 1 tablespoon fresh jalapeño, seeded and finely chopped
- ¼ cup fresh cilantro, chopped
- ¼ teaspoon cayenne pepper, ground
- 1 tablespoon lime zest, grated
- 2 teaspoons lime juice
- 1 teaspoon onion powder
- 2 cloves garlic, minced

JOHN says

If there's any vegetable you want to buy off the back of a truck, it's sweet, fresh Silver Queen corn. Peel back the top of the corn husk and make sure that the tops are moist and white. Steaming your corn traps in the sweetness and complements the lemony tang of cilantro and the heat of the jalapeño.

Steamed Salmon
with Creole Sauce

Serves 6

1. Fill Butterball® or Masterbuilt Fryer to the MAX fill line with water. Set to 375° F and bring to a boil. This will take approximately 15 to 20 minutes. Although cooking time on this recipe is short, water may need to be added if steamer is used for more than 60 minutes.

2. Rub olive oil on salmon steaks and sprinkle them with Butterball® Cajun Seasoning. Place salmon steaks in the basket and, using the drain clip, hook basket onto inner pot. (Note: Do not lower basket into water when steaming.) Cover and steam for 12 to 15 minutes.

3. Remove salmon from steamer. Plate salmon steaks and sprinkle with parsley. Top with Creole sauce and serve with lemon wedges.

Creole Sauce:

1. In a large skillet, heat butter over medium high heat until melted. Add tomatoes, onion, green pepper, celery, and garlic then sauté for 8 minutes, or until vegetables are tender. Add bouillon cube, pepper, oregano, basil, hot sauce, and bay leaves and bring to a boil. Reduce heat and simmer covered, for 20 minutes, stirring occasionally. Remove bay leaves just before serving. Makes 2 cups.

You'll Need:

- 6 (6 ounce) salmon steaks
- 1 tablespoon extra virgin olive oil
- ½ teaspoon Butterball Cajun Seasoning
- 2 tablespoons fresh parsley, chopped
- Lemon wedges

Creole Sauce:

- 3 tablespoons butter
- 1 (15 ounce) can diced tomatoes with roasted garlic and onion, undrained
- ⅔ cup yellow onion, chopped
- ⅔ cup green bell pepper, chopped
- ⅔ cup celery, chopped
- 2 teaspoons minced garlic
- 1 chicken-flavored bouillon cube
- ½ teaspoon coarsely ground black pepper
- ½ teaspoon oregano
- ½ teaspoon basil
- ¼ teaspoon hot sauce
- 2 bay leaves

STEAMED

JOHN *says*

Salmon has a slightly bolder flavor than other fish and this creole sauce complements it well. You may want to steam the steaks skin on and skin down. It helps hold the salmon together and makes it easier to lift steaks in and out of the basket. Pairs well with Steamed Vegetables. (See page 77 for recipe.)

Spiced Sweet Potatoes
with Ginger and Pears

Serves 4 to 8

1. Fill Butterball® or Masterbuilt Fryer to the MAX fill line with water. Set to 375° F and bring to a boil. This will take approximately 15 to 20 minutes. Although cooking time on this recipe is short, water may need to be added if steamer is used for more than 60 minutes.

2. Coat steamer basket with non-stick cooking spray and add the sweet potatoes. Using the drain clip, hook the basket onto the inner pot. (Note: Do not lower basket into water when steaming.) Cover and steam for 25 minutes, or until soft enough to mash.

3. In a medium skillet, sauté pears, butter, cinnamon, and nutmeg until pears caramelize, about 2 minutes.

4. Transfer steamed sweet potatoes to a large bowl and coarsely mash, adding cardamom, ginger, salt and pepper. Stir in the sautéed pears.

5. Place the mixture into a shallow casserole, and bake in a pre-heated 350° F oven, until heated through, 15 to 20 minutes.

You'll Need:

- 2 lbs. sweet potatoes, cut into ½- to 1-inch chunks
- 3 ripe pears, peeled, cored and diced
- 2 tablespoons butter
- ½ teaspoon cinnamon
- ¼ teaspoon nutmeg
- 1 teaspoon ground cardamom
- 2 teaspoons ginger, finely chopped
- ½ teaspoon salt
- ¼ teaspoon black pepper

JOHN says

Here's a full-flavored dish that's a perfect side for the holidays. The pears add a lot of sweetness, so you may want to balance it with a green vegetable like steamed green beans or zucchini.

Steamed Shrimp
with Seafood Spice Mix

Serves 4

1. Fill Butterball® or Masterbuilt Fryer to the MAX fill line with water. Set to 375° F and bring to a boil. This will take approximately 15 to 20 minutes. Although cooking time on this recipe is short, water may need to be added if steamer is used for more than 60 minutes.

2. In a large bowl add shrimp and sprinkle with the seasoning mix. Place shrimp in basket. Using the drain clip, hook basket onto the inner pot. (Note: Do not lower basket into water when steaming.) Cover and steam shrimp for 6 to 8 minutes or until shrimp turns pink. Serve the shrimp with lemon wedges and a dish of the spices or your favorite cocktail sauce for dipping.

You'll Need:
- 2 lbs. raw medium shrimp (21 to 30 count) shells on
- 1 medium or large lemon, cut into wedges

Seafood Spice Mix:
- 1 tablespoon chili powder
- 1 tablespoon paprika
- ¼ teaspoon cayenne pepper
- 1 bay leaf, finely ground
- ½ teaspoon dry mustard
- 1 teaspoon oregano, dried
- 1 teaspoon salt
- ½ teaspoon black pepper
- 1 teaspoon granulated sugar
- ½ teaspoon coriander seed, ground

JOHN *says*

This recipe is from the Eastern Shore of Maryland where the shrimp are doused with spices and steamed over boiling water (not boiled). Leave the shells on. I recommend easy peel, split back shrimp for less work and more time to serve and eat. To save time, replace the Seafood Spice Mix with Butterball® Cajun Seasoning.

New Zealand Mussels

Serves 4 to 6

1. Fill Butterball® or Masterbuilt Fryer to the MAX fill line with water. Set to 375° F and bring to a boil. This will take approximately 15 to 20 minutes. Although cooking time on this recipe is short, water may need to be added if steamer is used for more than 60 minutes.

2. In a medium-size skillet, combine olive oil, garlic, tomatoes, scallions, cilantro, crushed red pepper flakes, and salt. Sauté for 3 minutes, or until vegetables are tender.

3. Using heavy-duty aluminum foil, make a foil packet to line the steamer basket. Place mussels in the foil-lined basket and pour tomato mixture over them. Pour vinegar and clam juice next, then close packet and poke holes in top to let steam escape. Cover and steam for 8 minutes, or until mussels open. (Note: Do not lower basket into water when steaming.) Serve with lime wedges.

You'll Need:

- 2 tablespoons extra virgin olive oil
- 1 teaspoon garlic, minced
- 1 large tomato, seeded and diced
- 2 scallions, including green tops, finely chopped
- 1 tablespoon fresh cilantro, chopped
- ¼ teaspoon red pepper flakes
- ½ teaspoon sea salt
- 24 mussels, rinsed, scrubbed and de-bearded
- ¼ cup white wine vinegar
- ¾ cup clam juice
- 1 lime cut into wedges

JOHN *says*

Cleaning mussels can get pretty labor intensive, so choose carefully. Look for a label on the bag indicating how and where the mussels were cultivated. Avoid wild mussels and look for grit-free "rope cultured mussels." Pick through your mussels and if you find any open ones, tap them sharply on your kitchen counter. If they don't close immediately, discard them. You can use the dull side of a paring knife to pull off the beards. Serve with Steamed Vegetables and Steamed Sweet Corn. (See pages 77 and 82 for recipes.)

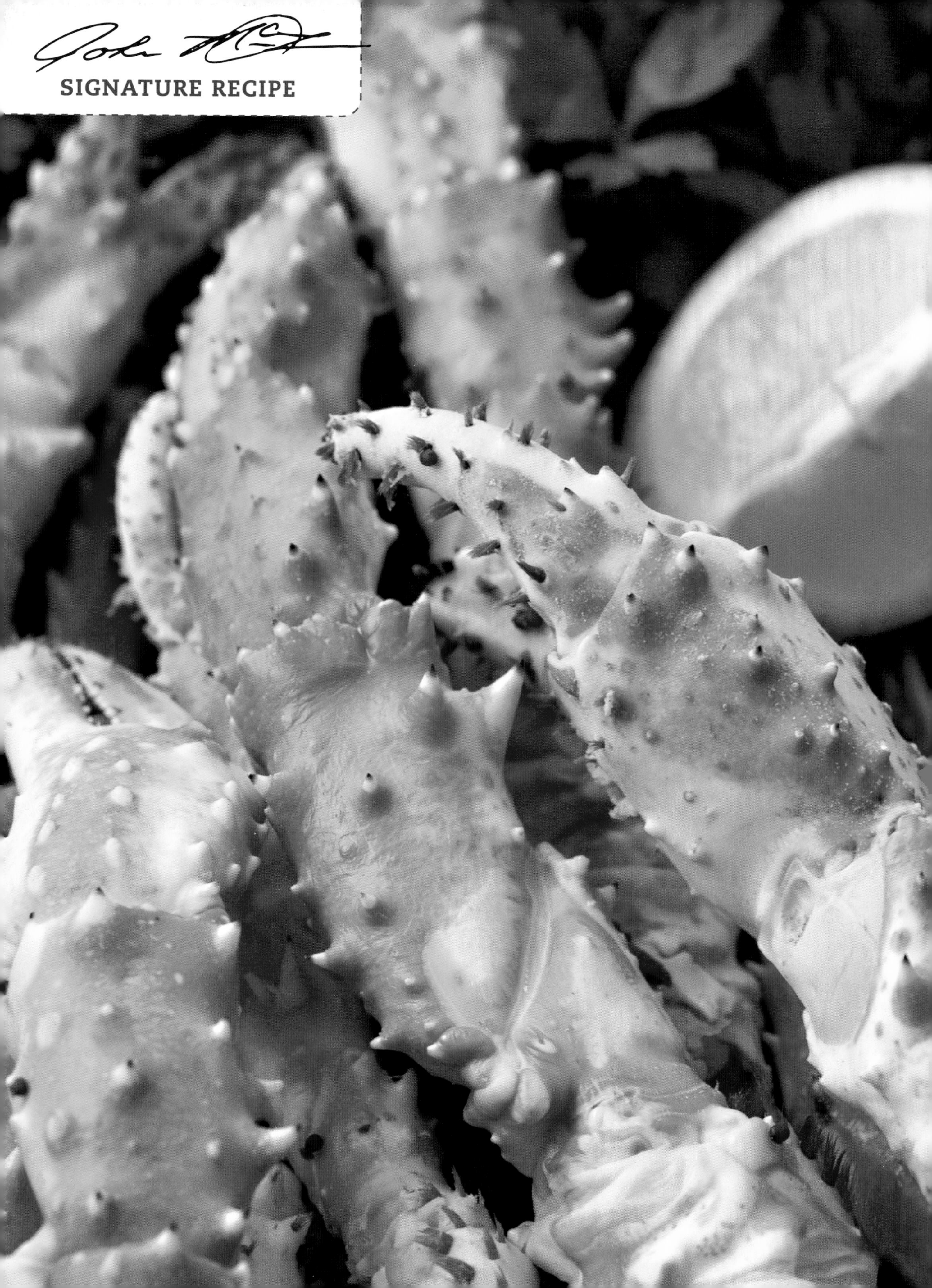

SIGNATURE RECIPE

Steamed Crab Legs

Serves 4

1. Fill Butterball® or Masterbuilt Fryer to the MAX fill line with water. Set to 375° F and bring to a boil. Add salt and crab boil. This will take approximately 15 to 20 minutes. Although cooking time on this recipe is short, water may need to be added if steamer is used for more than 60 minutes.

2. Add the crab legs to basket. Using the drain clip, hook basket onto the inner pot. (Note: Do not lower basket into water when steaming.) As the water starts to boil again, begin timing. Steam the crab legs for 15 to 20 minutes, until you begin to smell their aroma. Make sure not to overcook the legs. Remove from the heat and serve hot with melted butter and lemon wedges.

You'll Need:

- 1 ½ lbs. King Crab legs, split and thawed
- 1 tablespoon salt
- 1 tablespoon crab boil
- Juice of 1 lemon
- ½ cup (1 stick) butter, melted

JOHN says

Most crab legs have already been cooked and blast-frozen to secure their taste. If you buy frozen crab legs, thaw them overnight in your refrigerator, or if you're in a hurry they can be thawed under cold water to speed up the process.

Traditional English Pudding Dessert

Serves 6 to 8

1. Fill Butterball® or Masterbuilt Fryer to the MAX fill line with water. Set to 375° F and bring to a boil. This will take approximately 15 to 20 minutes. Water may need to be added if steamer is used for more than 60 minutes.

2. In a medium mixing bowl, cream the butter and sugar with an electric mixer. Slowly add in the flour, eggs, salt, and milk, continue to blend until batter is smooth.

3. Coat a 1-quart, heat-proof bowl with non-stick cooking spray. Put jam in the bottom of the bowl, pour and smooth batter over the jam. Cover with foil, tucking the edges carefully around the rim of the bowl.

4. Place covered bowl in the basket. Using the drain clip, hook basket onto the inner pot. (Note: Do not lower basket into water when steaming.) Cover and steam for 75 minutes, then carefully remove from steamer, and invert pudding onto a serving plate. Serve warm with vanilla ice cream, fruit, or extra jam.

You'll Need:
- ½ cup butter, room temperature
- ⅔ cup sugar
- 1 ½ cups self-rising flour
- 2 large eggs, beaten
- ½ teaspoon salt
- 4 tablespoons milk
- 4 tablespoons jam, any flavor

STEAMED

JOHN *says*

Pick a dish that fits in the basket. Keep the lid closed and don't peek, let it steam for 75 minutes. This dessert is not only easy but surprisingly good, especially with your favorite vanilla ice cream or drizzled with sweetened condensed milk!

Steamed Chicken and Vegetables
Serves 2

1. Thinly slice the chicken and set aside. In a medium bowl, combine 3 tablespoons orange juice and 1 tablespoon soy sauce. Add chicken and marinate for 8 hours, or place overnight in the refrigerator.

2. Fill Butterball® or Masterbuilt Fryer to the MAX fill line with water. Set to 375° F and bring to a boil. This will take approximately 15 to 20 minutes. Although cooking time on this recipe is short, water may need to be added if steamer is used for more than 60 minutes.

3. Put mushrooms, carrots, and celery in basket. Place marinated chicken on top of vegetables. Using drain clip, hook basket onto the inner pot. (Note: Do not lower basket into water when steaming.) Cover and steam approximately 20 minutes, or until chicken is cooked through.

4. Add snow peas and continue to steam until peas turn bright green, for 3 to 5 minutes.

Sauce:
1. In a medium saucepan, combine remaining orange juice and soy sauce with the water, oyster sauce, cornstarch, and sesame oil. Cook in a saucepan over medium heat until thickened, stirring continuously for about 5 minutes. Serve chicken and vegetables over rice and drizzle with sauce. Makes 1-½ cups.

You'll Need:
- 2 boneless skinless chicken breasts, thinly sliced
- 5 tablespoons orange juice
- 2 tablespoons light soy sauce
- ½ lb. fresh mushrooms, halved
- 2 carrots, peeled and sliced at an angle
- 2 celery stalks, sliced at an angle
- ¼ lb. fresh snow peas, strings removed
- 2 cups freshly cooked rice

Sauce:
- 1 cup water
- 2 tablespoons oyster sauce
- 1 tablespoon cornstarch
- 1 ½ teaspoons Oriental sesame oil

JOHN *says*

To capture more flavor and to keep the little snow peas from gettin' away, line your basket with aluminum foil. This recipe is healthy, easy and *Dadgum Good!*

Low Country Boil

Serves 4 to 6

1. Fill Butterball® or Masterbuilt Fryer to the MAX fill line with water. (NOTE: If using a seasoning bag, place bag in basket.) Set heat to 375° F and bring to a boil. This will take approximately 20 to 25 minutes.

2. Add whole potatoes to basket and lower carefully into boiling water; boil for 12 minutes.

3. Add corn to the potatoes, and boil an additional 9 minutes.

4. Add sausage to the potatoes and corn, continuing to boil for 9 more minutes.

5. Lastly, add shrimp. Boil for an additional 3 to 5 minutes until shrimp are pink. Total cooking time for the boil is 33 to 35 minutes. Lift the basket from the hot water slowly, hooking the drain clip on the basket into drain clip mounting hole. Allow Low Country Boil to drain, and serve hot.

You'll Need:

- ½ cup Butterball® Cajun Seasoning (or your favorite seafood boil seasoning or bag)
- 2 lbs. of whole new potatoes
- 8 to 12 pieces of short-ear corn
- 2 lbs. pre-cooked smoked sausage (½ to 1-inch thick slices)
- 2 lbs. shrimp, preferably split and deveined

Dipping Sauce:

- ½ cup butter
- 4 medium cloves garlic, minced

Dipping Sauce:

1. In a medium saucepan, melt butter over a low heat. Add minced garlic and mix. Drizzle butter sauce over each plate or serve on the side.

JOHN *says*

Nothing is better or easier for large and small crowds than our Low Country Boil. For a splash-free cooking experience, I recommend you hook the basket as you add each ingredient. If you like, you can substitute some of the shrimp with crawfish. Complete the experience and have a little fun by dumping the boil out on newspaper for a true "grab 'n' growl" – no forks required!

BOILED

Shrimp Boil

Serves 4 to 6

1. Fill Butterball® or Masterbuilt Fryer to the MAX fill line with water. Set heat to boiling at 375° F and bring to a boil. This will take approximately 20 to 25 minutes.

2. Place liquid shrimp boil, Butterball® Cajun Seasoning, and lemon juice into boiling water.

3. Add shrimp into the basket and lower basket into the boiling water. Cook for 8 to 10 minutes or until shrimp turns pink. Drain and serve with seafood sauce.

Sauce:

1. In a small bowl, combine the ketchup, onion, horseradish, lemon juice, and tarragon. Serve with your favorite seafood. Makes 1 cup.

You'll Need:

- 2 teaspoons liquid shrimp boil
- 2 teaspoons Butterball Cajun Seasoning
- ½ cup freshly squeezed lemon juice
- 2 to 5 lbs. medium shrimp

Sauce:

- 1 cup ketchup
- 3 tablespoons onion, grated
- 3 tablespoons horseradish
- 2 tablespoons fresh lemon juice
- 2 tablespoons fresh tarragon, chopped

JOHN *says*

I love shrimp cooked a lot of different ways. This recipe is quick, easy and has a great Cajun flare. I recommend you get the easy-peel, split-back shrimp to make serving and eating easy.

Boiled Lobster
with Citrus-Herb Butter Sauce

Serves 2

1. Fill Butterball® or Masterbuilt Fryer with water to the MAX line. Set heat to 375° F and bring to a boil. This will take approximately 20 to 25 minutes. Place lobster in basket and lower into water. Cover and boil for 15 minutes or until internal temperature reaches 140° F.

2. While lobster is boiling, combine sauce ingredients in a small saucepan over medium heat. Cook 3 to 4 minutes or until butter is melted. Makes ¾ cup sauce.

You'll Need:
- 2 (1 ½ lb.) live lobsters

Sauce:
- ½ cup butter
- 1 teaspoon lemon rind, grated
- 1 teaspoon lemon juice
- 1 teaspoon orange rind, grated
- 1 tablespoon orange juice
- 2 tablespoons fresh chives, chopped
- 1 tablespoon fresh parsley, chopped
- ¼ teaspoon cayenne pepper
- ¼ teaspoon salt

JOHN *says*

Whether you pull a lobster straight out of the tank in the store or directly out of the sea, its tail should be flapping. If it's limp, that's a sign of a soon-to-be-dead lobster. A lobster with a softer shell has recently molted and is likely to have more water weight and less meat. Be ready to boil your lobster as soon as you get home. A 1 ½ pound lobster should cook for about 15 minutes, while a 4 to 5 pounder should cook for 22 to 24 minutes, or until the body is bright red.

Southern Boiled Peanuts

Serves 5 to 10

1. Soak peanuts in a large pot filled with water overnight. Drain the next morning. Since raw peanuts will float, you can use an appropriate-sized plate to weigh them down and keep them submerged.

2. Fill Butterball® or Masterbuilt Fryer with water to the MAX line. Set heat to 375° F and bring to a boil. This will take approximately 20 to 25 minutes.

3. Add salt and seasoning to the boiling water. Place peanuts in the steamer basket and lower into water. Reduce heat to 250° F, and boil 4 to 6 hours, or until peanuts are cooked to desired tenderness. (Note: Check water level if boiling for more than 60 minutes, and add more water as needed when evaporation occurs.)

You'll Need:
- 1 to 3 lbs. raw peanuts
- ¼ to ⅓ cup salt
- ⅙ to ¼ cup Butterball® Cajun Fried Turkey Seasoning

BOILED

JOHN *says*

Boiled peanuts are so popular in the Carolinas, Georgia, Northern Florida, Alabama and Mississippi, you'll always find roadside stands offering fresh boiled peanuts. Some folks say it's an acquired taste, but once you've tried them you'll be hooked. Now you only have to travel to the kitchen to feed your craving for these Southern treats.

The Masterbuilt Story
as told by John McLemore

When I met Tonya, it was on a blind date arranged by our parents. No joke. I instantly knew she was the one for me. Tonya, however, wasn't buying the pitch, because my reputation preceded me. Now, I've always been a natural salesman, the kind of guy who can sell an anchor to a drowning man. But this time my skills weren't working. However, I somehow convinced her to have dinner at my house. So I boiled up some fresh lobster and grilled steaks for our first date. Little did I realize, it was my cooking—not my sports car—that would ultimately seal the deal. I'm not about to claim that a lobster prepared in one of our products helped win Tonya's heart, but it certainly didn't hurt.

Don later met Lynne, who succeeded in handily seducing him with her baking skills; skills that Don fell in love with and used, as she tested each new product in the coming years. Also, as I said earlier, Don and I did everything together and so did the new members of the family. We built our homes next to each other, we traveled together and we started having our children around the same time. Tonya and I had Brooke in May, 1990; Don and Lynne had Blake in October, 1990. We had John in July, 1992; they had Brett in July, 1994. We had Bailey in February, 1998; then they had Trevor in November, 1998. It may not have been planned that way, but we managed to round out our families. As the kids were growing up— from 1996 to 2006—Lynne took on the role of CFO of the company. Tonya was a second grade teacher at our local elementary school from 1989 to 1999.

In 1991, our facility burned to the ground, but what emerged from the ashes was a single-minded focus that made Don and I more determined than ever to succeed. We have faced many trials and God has always helped us through. Our success has been built on not only hard work, but the blessings and protection of God—a core belief that Don and I still share to this day.

Top:
Tonya and John on their wedding day

Below Top:
Lynne and Don on their wedding day

Bottom Left:
John with daughter Brooke

Bottom Right:
John and son, J-Mac– third generation working at Masterbuilt

Top Left:
Don says, "Bro... save me a rib"

Top Right:
Don, Bill, Donna, Dad, Mom and Bubba
Everyone but me!

Below:
Masterbuilt introduces the Electric Turkey Fryer in 2003

Bottom:
Don and John Deep-Fry turkeys in 2003

If anything has enabled us to endure adversity, it's our ability to work together and our belief in placing family ahead of business. Throughout thirty-odd years in business, our roles in the company have always complemented each other. So far (knock on wood), we have never had a single disagreement.

As partners, Don and I have determined our respective strengths and learned how to divide and conquer. As the guy who had sold the family's product from the age of eight, I naturally fell into the role of sales and promotion, while Don focused on distribution and operations.

Those talents would be put to good use as we embarked on an aggressive direct marketing campaign to promote Masterbuilt's complete range of products.

By 1994, we had produced two instructional cooking videos, entitled "Masterbuilt's Cooking Made Simple." (For some great tips, look for them on Masterbuilt.com, or YouTube.com.) It's scary to see how much younger we looked back then.

By 1998, our reputation for quality and innovation at Masterbuilt was known throughout ten Southeastern states. Not satisfied with our efforts, Don and I resolved to double the size of the company in five years through aggressive advertising and expanded distribution to national retailers.

In 2001, with the help of one of our most dedicated employees, Danny East, we came up with our most ambitious product idea: the world's first Electric Turkey Fryer—one that would be safe and suitable for indoor use. Two years and several prototypes later, the patented CSA safety-certified Indoor Electric Turkey Fryer was finally ready to carry the Masterbuilt name. Once again, we had realized a goal of developing a product no other company had ever created.

Continued on page 156

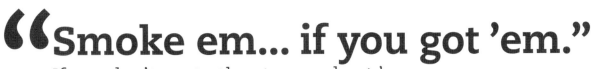

"Smoke em... if you got 'em."

If you don't, go to the store and get 'em.

Masterbuilt's Electric Smoker is perfect, whether you're a novice smoking for the first time, or a seasoned smoker who wants to smoke food without the effort or attention that smoking typically requires. Here's why customers call it the best smoker for the money:

· With 4 smoking racks, it's spacious and robust enough to smoke up to 50 lbs. of meat at a time.

· No need to constantly worry about keeping the smoker at the right temperature. A built-in thermostat lets you set your preferred temperature and time, the easy-load wood tray keeps you from having to open the door.

· This smoker requires relatively small amounts of wood and enables you to smoke smaller batches without the hassle of using propane or charcoal.

TIPS ···

· Take the time to season your new smoker before your first meal. Fill your wood chip tray with a handful of wood chips. Set your smoker to the highest temp setting, open the air vents and allow it to smoke for about 2 hours, adding wood chips again 2 times during this process. This will remove any residue from the manufacturing process.

· During the smoking process, if internal food temperatures get close to the desired target early, you can wrap the food in aluminum foil to retain the moisture then reduce the smoker temperature until mealtime.

· Wet ribs or dry ribs? It's all a matter of preference. For wet ribs, apply your favorite BBQ sauce and wrap with aluminum foil during the last hour of smoking. For a dry rib, use your favorite dry-rub seasoning. Don't let the fact that your smoker has a water bowl confuse you. Filling this water bowl does not give you a "wet" rib, it's just a way of infusing more flavor into the rib (i.e. fruit juice diluted 50/50 with water).

· The most commonly used wood chips for smoking are hickory and mesquite, which are easy to find in most grocery stores. If you want to try something different, keep an eye out for apple or pecan wood chips, which add a unique, milder smoked flavor.

Smoked Pork Butt

Serves 4 to 8

1. Combine apple cider vinegar and water in the Masterbuilt smoker's water pan. Load the wood tray with one small handful of wood chips and preheat the smoker to 225° F.

2. Trim excess fat from pork butt. In a small bowl, combine the Greek seasoning, black pepper, and red pepper. Rub mixture on all sides of pork butt. Place butt in smoker and smoke for 6 to 8 hours, or until internal temperature reaches 160° F.

You'll Need:

- 1 cup apple cider vinegar
- 1 cup water
- 1 (5 to 7 lb.) pork butt
- 2 tablespoons Greek seasoning
- 2 tablespoons black pepper
- ½ teaspoon red pepper

SMOKED

JOHN *says*

You can purchase your pork butt with the bone in or boneless. I like both. With the bone in, you get a great flavor, but you may need to smoke it a tad longer. If I am making sandwiches, I like to use a boneless butt and cut the meat into inch-thick slices for a *Dadgum Good* BBQ sandwich.

Smoked Asparagus

Serves 4 to 6

1. Load the wood tray with one small handful of wood chips and preheat Masterbuilt smoker to 225° F.

2. Melt the butter in a small saucepan, stir in the garlic and cook over low heat until garlic is just tender, about 10 minutes. Remove from the heat and mix in the lemon juice, salt, and black pepper. Arrange the onions in a medium-size baking dish. Spread asparagus spears over the onions. Drizzle the butter and garlic mixture over the asparagus.

3. Place the uncovered baking dish on the top grate of the preheated smoker. Smoke until asparagus is tender, about 1 ½ to 2 hours.

You'll Need:
- 4 tablespoons butter
- 4 cloves garlic, thinly sliced
- 2 tablespoons freshly squeezed lemon juice
- $\frac{1}{16}$ teaspoon salt
- ¼ teaspoon black pepper
- 1 medium yellow onion, thinly sliced
- 1 ½ lbs. asparagus, trimmed

JOHN *says*

Make sure you snap the ends off the asparagus. Stick to the allotted smoking time; too much smoke will make the asparagus bitter.

Pork Loin (Porchetta)
with Fiery Sweet Red Pepper Sauce

Serves 6 to 8

Porchetta:

1. Place loin on cutting board running lengthwise away from you. Using a boning knife (a chef's knife will do, but a boning or filet knife is a bit easier), hold the knife at a 45-degree angle and cut a ¾-inch deep flap, lengthwise, starting at the top of the loin. Fold the flap you just cut back and continue to make additional cuts of the same depth and length, unrolling the loin as you go. You should end up with a flat piece of meat that is a uniform ¾ to 1-inch thickness.

2. In a medium saucepan, bring water to boil. Add salt, sugar, garlic, and peppercorns, stirring continuously until everything is dissolved. Remove from heat and add apple cider. Set aside to cool. After brine is cool, add grape juice.

3. Combine brine and loin in a resealable plastic storage bag. Place bag into a baking dish and refrigerate overnight.

Stuffing:

1. Load the wood tray with one small handful of wood chips and preheat smoker to 225° F.

2. Remove loin from brine and place flat on a cutting board. Lightly salt and pepper and set aside.

3. In a large skillet, heat olive oil; add the onion and cook until translucent. Add ground pork, sage, fennel seeds, rosemary, basil, thyme, salt, pepper, garlic, and pine nuts. Cook until mixture is lightly browned, then remove from heat and set aside to cool. Once cooled, add beaten eggs and mix well.

4. Spread the mixture over the pork loin, leaving ½-inch edge clean on all sides. Roll the meat like a jelly roll. Tie with butcher's twine and place in the middle rack of the smoker. Reduce temperature to 225° F and add additional wood each hour. Smoke at 225° F until the internal temperature reaches 160° F, approximately, 2 hours. Remove and allow to rest for 10 to 20 minutes before serving.

Fiery Sweet Roasted Red Peppers: (Optional)

1. In a medium-sized mixing bowl, combine peppers, sugar, pepper flakes, and garlic. Cover and let stand overnight at room temperature before serving.

You'll Need:

- 1 (3 to 4 lb.) pork loin, cut jelly roll style
- 2 cups water
- ½ cup kosher salt
- ½ cup brown sugar
- 5 cloves garlic, crushed
- 1 tablespoon whole peppercorns
- 4 ½ cups apple cider
- 2 ½ cups red grape juice

Stuffing:

- Salt and black pepper
- ¼ cup extra virgin olive oil
- 1 medium onion, diced
- 1 lb. ground pork
- 1 tablespoon sage, chopped
- 2 tablespoons fennel seeds
- 2 tablespoons rosemary
- 1 tablespoon basil, dried
- 1 tablespoon thyme, dried
- ½ teaspoon salt
- 2 tablespoons black pepper
- 5 cloves garlic, minced
- ¼ cup pine nuts, toasted and ground (optional)
- 2 eggs, beaten

Fiery Sweet Roasted Red Peppers:

- 1 (12 ounce) jar roasted red peppers, cut into strips
- 1 cup sugar
- 2 tablespoons crushed red pepper flakes for heat
- 2 cloves garlic, crushed

SMOKED

Smoked Potato Salad

Serves 4 to 6

1. Load the wood tray with one small handful of wood chips and preheat the smoker to 225° F.

2. Peel potatoes and place them in a large saucepot with water to cover and boil for 20 minutes, until just tender. Drain potatoes, and dry them, on a plate layered with paper towels.

3. Place potatoes directly on the smoker racks and close smoker door. Reduce heat to 200° F and add more wood chips every 45 minutes. Keep potatoes in smoker for 2 hours. Remove potatoes from smoker and dice them for the salad.

4. In a large bowl mix onion, pickles, boiled eggs, mayonnaise, vinegar, mustard, salt, and pepper to taste. Add diced potatoes to the mixture, cover and chill salad in the refrigerator for several hours.

Suggested Wood Chips For Smoking:
Mesquite

You'll Need:
- 1 ½ lbs. russet potatoes, peeled
- ½ cup red onion, finely diced
- ½ cup crisp tart pickles, chopped
- 3 hard boiled eggs, coarsely chopped
- ⅓ cup light mayonnaise
- 2 tablespoons cider vinegar
- 1 tablespoon Dijon mustard
- Salt and black pepper

JOHN *says*

Smoking is not just for meat, it's great for all types of vegetables and even some fruits. Don't forget our Four-Cheese Smoked Mac 'n' Cheese (See page 112 for recipe), which I consider (along with most kids) to be a vegetable, too!

BBQ Beans Smoker Style

Serves 4

1. Soak beans overnight in enough cold water to cover, plus an extra 3-inches of water above beans. The next day, drain and rinse beans and place in a large stockpot. Add enough cold water to cover, plus an extra 3-inches of water, and bring to a boil over high heat. Reduce the heat and simmer until beans are almost tender, about 1 hour. Drain, and combine beans, onion, sugar, ketchup, vinegar, molasses, mustard, chili powder, garlic, cayenne, salt, and five cups of water in a large 9 by 13-inch aluminum baking pan.

2. Load the wood tray with one small handful of wood chips and preheat the smoker to 225° F.

3. Place pan on the bottom rack of the smoker and cook for 45 minutes. Stir occasionally, checking to see that the juice gets thicker, but not too dry. If it becomes dry add a little water.

You'll Need:

- 1 lb. dried navy beans, rinsed
- 1 medium onion, chopped
- ½ cup light brown sugar, tightly packed
- ½ cup ketchup
- ⅓ cup red wine vinegar
- ¼ cup molasses
- 2 tablespoons Dijon mustard
- 1 tablespoon chili powder
- 2 teaspoons garlic, minced
- ½ teaspoon cayenne pepper
- Kosher salt

JOHN says

To give this dish a unique flavor, smoke the beans on a rack underneath a pork butt. The drippings from the pork butt enhance the smoky flavor. The pork butt will shed most of its fat during the first few hours. Put the baked beans in the smoker 45 minutes before you remove the butt and you'll get the benefit of the pork flavor without too much fat. Stir the beans well before serving.

SMOKED

Four-Cheese Smoked Mac 'n' Cheese

Serves 4 to 6

You'll Need:

- 1 (16 ounce) package elbow macaroni
- ¼ cup butter
- ¼ cup all purpose flour
- 3 cups milk
- 1 (8 ounces) cream cheese, cut into large chunks
- 1 teaspoon salt
- ½ teaspoon black pepper
- 2 cups (8 ounces) extra sharp Cheddar cheese, shredded
- 2 cups (8 ounces) Gouda cheese shredded
- 1 cup (4 ounces) Parmesan cheese, shredded

JOHN *says*

I continue to be surprised at the rave reviews we receive every time we make our Smoked Mac 'n' Cheese. The smoke-infused flavor knocks everyone's socks off! If you are in a hurry, purchase ready-made mac 'n' cheese, top it with an extra layer of your favorite cheese, and get results almost as good as homemade.

1. Load the wood tray with one small handful of wood chips and preheat the smoker to 225° F.

2. Cook pasta according to package instructions. In a medium saucepan, melt butter, and whisk flour into the butter. Cook over medium heat for 2 minutes, until sauce is bubbly and thick. Whisk in milk and bring to a boil. Cook 5 minutes until thickened. Stir in cream cheese until mixture is smooth. Add salt and pepper.

3. In a large bowl, combine 1 cup Cheddar, 1 cup Gouda cheese, Parmesan cheese, pasta, and cream sauce. Spoon mixture into an 11 by 9 ½-inch aluminum roasting pan coated with nonstick cooking spray. Sprinkle top with remaining Cheddar cheese and Gouda cheese.

4. Place in smoker and cook 1 hour at 225° F, until brown, bubbly and delicious.

Smoked Salmon

Serves 4 to 6

1. Load the wood tray with one small handful of wood chips and preheat the smoker to 220° F.

2. Wash and pat dry the salmon filets. Place filets on baking sheet, skin side down. In a small bowl, combine fresh dill and black pepper. Sprinkle each filet with the pepper and dill mixture.

3. Thinly slice one lemon. Completely cover each filet with the onion and then the lemon slices. Sprinkle each filet with the juice of the other lemon.

4. Place baking sheet on bottom rack and smoke for 30 minutes, or until salmon meat is flaky.

Suggested Wood Chips For Smoking:
Hickory, Apple or Pecan

You'll Need:

- 3 to 4 salmon filets with skin
- ½ teaspoon fresh dill
- ½ teaspoon black pepper
- 2 lemons
- 1 onion, thinly sliced

JOHN *says*

Most dishes are only as good as the ingredients that go into them and this is especially true for salmon. It spoils quickly and if it's not flash-frozen or properly iced, it develops a fishy odor. Here are a couple of things to look for. The eyes should be bright and clear with no signs of cloudiness. The flesh should be firm to the touch. Press your finger into the fish. If it's fresh, it will spring back to its original shape. If it doesn't spring back, it may be spoiled.

SMOKED

Game Hens
with Asian Citrus Baste
Serves 8

1. Season hens with 1 teaspoon of salt and 1 teaspoon of pepper. Split each game hen in half. In a medium bowl, thoroughly mix garlic, onions, brown sugar, cilantro, 1 teaspoon pepper, lemon juice, lime juice, orange juice, soy sauce, and hot sauce. Reserve 1 cup for basting.

2. Pour the remainder over hens and marinate for 6 to 8 hours in the refrigerator.

3. Load the wood tray with one small handful of wood chips and preheat the smoker to 225° F. Place hens in the smoker and smoke for 1 ½ hours to 1 hour 45 minutes, or until the internal temperature of the hens is 165° F. Using the cup of marinade, baste hens several times during smoking.

You'll Need:
- 4 game hens
- 1 teaspoon salt
- 2 teaspoons black pepper
- 3 cloves garlic, minced
- 3 green onions, minced
- 2 tablespoons brown sugar (firmly packed)
- 2 tablespoons cilantro, chopped
- 1 fresh large lemon, juiced
- 1 fresh large lime, juiced
- 1 cup fresh orange juice
- ¼ cup soy sauce
- 1 teaspoon hot sauce (Tabasco, or your favorite brand)

JOHN *says*

Game hens are more popular than most people know. They are almost always available at your local supermarket. A game hen is merely a small, young chicken. They are incredibly tender and a sure crowd pleaser. Check out our recipe for Cornish Game Hens (See page 59 for recipe).

Smoked Haute Dogs and Mustard

Serves 6

1. Load the wood tray with one small handful of wood chips and preheat the smoker to 225° F. Place 6 bratwursts on the top shelf of the smoker. Smoke for 1 to 1 ½ hours or until internal temperature reaches 160° F.

Mustard Sauce:

1. Heat oil in a large skillet. Sauté onions and green peppers over medium-low heat, stirring frequently, for 10 minutes, or until onions are golden brown.

2. Add the garlic and celery seeds, and continue cooking for 5 minutes. Stir in the Dijon mustard, and cook 3 more minutes to blend flavors. Serve immediately, or refrigerate to serve at a later time.

You'll Need:
- 6 bratwursts

Mustard Sauce:
- 3 tablespoons vegetable oil
- 1 large onion, coarsely diced
- 1 large green pepper, coarsely diced
- 2 cloves garlic, minced
- ½ teaspoon celery seeds
- ¼ cup Dijon mustard

Suggested Wood Chips For Smoking:

Hickory

JOHN says

Instead of simply grilling ordinary dogs, smoke some brats, then slather them with our delicious homemade mustard and you'll turn a hot dog into a haute dog. If you are short on time, these brats are also great with store-bought spicy brown mustard.

SMOKED

Super Smokers Sweet and Spicy Chicken Wings

Serves 4 to 6

1. In a small bowl, mix together the black pepper, onion powder, chili powder, garlic powder, and seasoned salt. Place the chicken wings in a large resealable bag. Pour the dry rub into the bag and shake to coat the wings well. Marinate for at least 30 minutes at room temperature, or up to 24 hours in the refrigerator.

2. Load the wood tray with one small handful of wood chips and preheat the smoker to 225° F. Place the wings on the top rack of the smoker, and cook for 25 to 30 minutes. Turn wings and cook for another 25 to 30 minutes, or until done.

3. While the wings are cooking, mix the honey, BBQ sauce, and apple juice together in a small saucepan. Cook over medium heat until warmed through. Remove the wings from the smoker and place in a disposable aluminum foil pan. Pour the warm sauce over the wings and toss to coat evenly. Return pan to smoker on middle rack and cook wings for another 25 minutes. Remove from the smoker and serve immediately.

Suggested Wood Chips For Smoking:

Apple or Pecan

You'll Need:
- 2 ½ tablespoons black pepper
- 1 tablespoon onion powder
- 1 tablespoon chili powder
- 1 tablespoon garlic powder
- 1 tablespoon seasoned salt
- 5 lbs. chicken wings, rinsed and dried
- 1 cup honey
- ½ cup hot BBQ sauce
- 3 tablespoons apple juice

SMOKED

JOHN *says*

These wings are super *Dadgum* spicy, so you can tone it down by cutting the black pepper in half and using a mild BBQ sauce. The honey and spices blend well for a unique flavor.

Turkey Salad
with Hazelnuts

Serves 2 to 4

You'll Need:

- 1 cup kosher salt
- 1 cup brown sugar
- ½ cup maple syrup
- 2 quarts apple juice
- 2 quarts water
- 1 (3 to 6 lb.) turkey breast

Salad:

- 1 cup green onions, chopped
- ¾ cup celery, chopped
- ⅓ cup mayonnaise
- 3 tablespoons fresh thyme, chopped
- 2 tablespoons lemon juice
- 6 tablespoons extra virgin olive oil
- 3 tablespoons white wine vinegar
- Salt and black pepper
- 1 (8 ounce) package mixed baby greens
- 2 ⅓ cups dried cherries, chopped (optional)
- ½ cup toasted hazelnuts, coarsely chopped

1. In a large container, combine the salt, brown sugar, syrup, apple juice and water. Mix the brine well. Place turkey in brine and refrigerate for 12 to 24 hours.

2. Load the wood tray with one small handful of wood chips and preheat the smoker to 250° F. Remove the turkey breast from brine and pat dry with paper towels. Reduce smoker temperature to 225° F. Place the turkey breast in the smoker and cook for 25 to 30 minutes per pound, or until inside meat temperature reaches 165° F. Remove turkey breast from smoker and let rest for 15 minutes before carving.

Salad:

1. In a medium bowl, mix sliced or chopped turkey, green onions, celery, mayonnaise, 2 tablespoons of thyme, and lemon juice.

2. To make the vinaigrette, whisk oil, vinegar, and the remaining thyme in a large mixing bowl. Season with salt and pepper.

3. Add greens to the vinaigrette mixture and toss. Divide among plates.

4. Top greens with cherries and nuts then serve.

JOHN *says*

This turkey is also great served by itself. For the salad, you can substitute dried cranberries for dried cherries if you want. To add an extra layer of flavor, toast the hazelnuts in a hot skillet for a few minutes.

Smoked Fish Omelette

Serves 2

1. Load the wood tray with one small handful of wood chips and preheat the smoker to 225° F. Smoke the fish at 225° F for 2 to 3 hours. Remove fish and flake apart with a fork.

2. In a medium bowl, beat the eggs, heavy cream, and milk together with salt and pepper. In a large non-stick skillet, melt butter and add the egg mixture. Cook for 6 minutes, lifting up sides of the omelette with a spatula to let egg liquid run out and set.

3. Add the flaked pieces of smoked fish, cheese, and onion on one half of the egg mixture. Fold egg over the top of fish mixture and remove from pan. Serve hot.

Suggested Wood Chips For Smoking:
Hickory

You'll Need:

- 1 (8 ounce) fish filet (preferably tilapia)
- 6 large eggs, beaten
- ½ cup of heavy cream
- 2 cups milk
- 1 teaspoon salt
- 1 teaspoon black pepper
- 2 tablespoons butter
- 1 cup (or more, to taste) grated sharp Cheddar cheese
- ¼ cup green onion, chopped

JOHN says

If you would like, you can smoke your fish the night before, which is actually where this recipe idea came from. We are always thinking of new ways to enjoy our leftovers. Smoked fish for dinner and a delicious omelette the next morning. Sounds *Dadgum Good* to me! And, if you're thinking "Really?" about fish in an omelette, let me assure you, it's great.

SMOKED

Smoked Prime Rib

Serves 4 to 6

1. Place prime rib in a large pan. In a small bowl, combine all dry ingredients and mix well. Season roast with the mixture and let stand for 30 to 45 minutes. Load the wood tray with one small handful of wood chips and preheat the smoker to 250° F.

2. Place roast, fat side up, directly on rack in smoker. Reduce temperature to 225° F and add more wood chips. Add extra wood chips every 1 to 1 ½ hours during cooking time.

3. Using meat thermometer to check temperature, cook until desired temperature is reached. (See temperatures below. Remember, meat will continue to cook for a few minutes when taken out of the smoker and covered with aluminum foil.)

4. Once you have removed the prime rib, cover it with foil and let it rest for 15 to 20 minutes before cutting. This will help keep prime rib warm and juicy.

Doneness:
125° F Rare
135° F Medium Rare
145° F Medium
155° F Medium Well
165° F Well Done (I don't recommend Well Done for a prime rib.) For medium rare to medium the cooking time is approximately 4 to 6 hours. (1 hour per pound.)

You'll Need:
- 1 (4 to 6 lbs.) prime rib roast
- ¼ tablespoon onion powder
- ⅛ tablespoon garlic powder
- 1 tablespoon black pepper
- 1 tablespoon white pepper
- 1 tablespoon paprika
- 1 tablespoon red pepper
- 1 tablespoon kosher salt

JOHN *says*

Purchase a boneless rib roast (a bone-in roast adds flavor, but needs to smoke a little longer). This is one of my favorite recipes and it gets rave reviews. Most people say it is the BEST *Dadgum* prime rib they have ever had.

SIGNATURE RECIPE

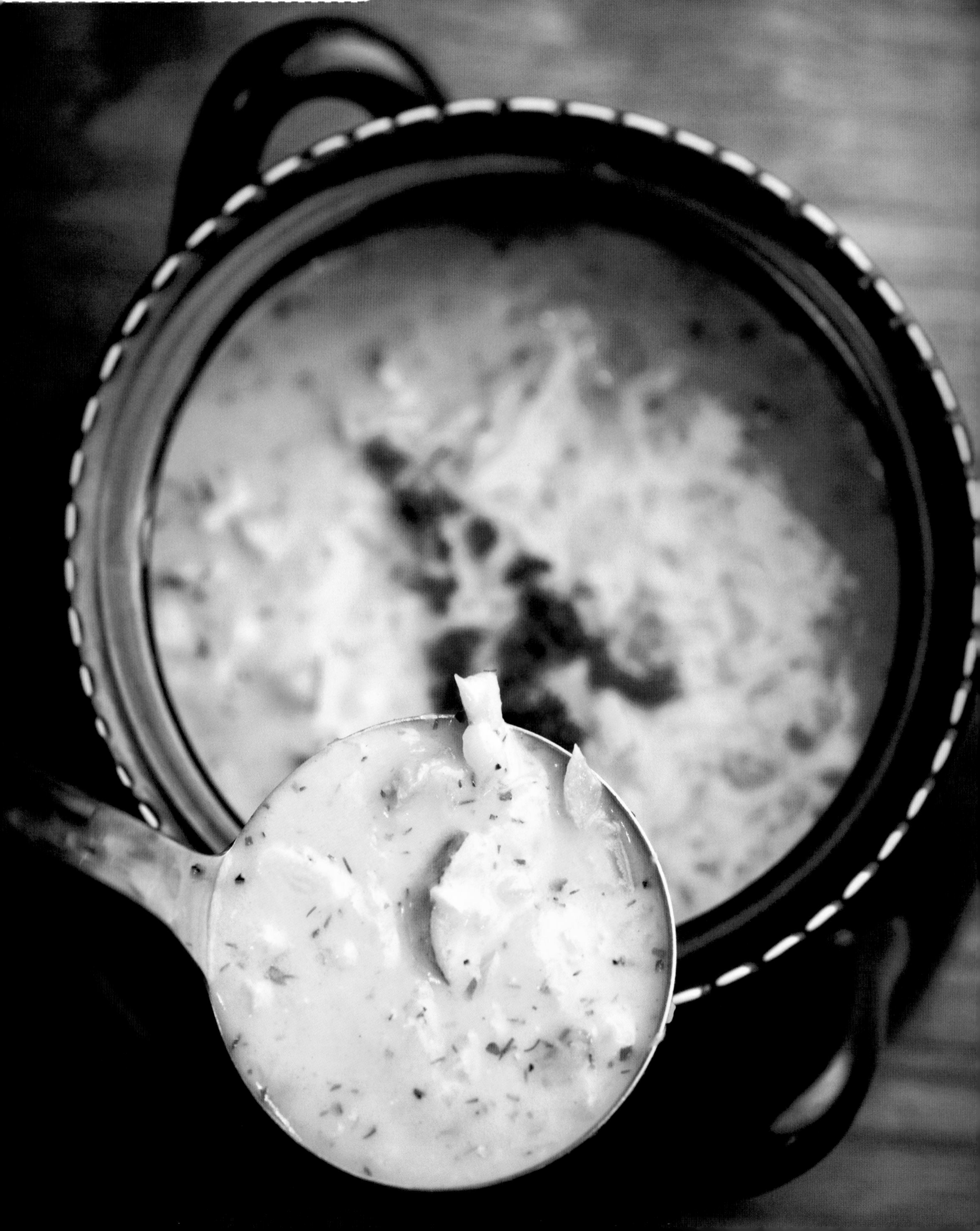

Smoked Salmon Chowder

Serves 4 to 6

1. Load the wood tray with one small handful of wood chips and preheat the smoker to 225° F.

2. Reduce smoker temp to 200° F and place salmon directly on rack. Smoke for 40 minutes at 200° F, or until internal temperature reaches 145° F.

3. In a large stockpot, combine the butter, olive oil, onion, garlic, and celery. Cook over medium-high heat for 8 to 10 minutes, or until the onions are transparent. Sprinkle flour over the mixture and stir well to make a dry roux. Gradually add the water and stir until liquid thickens slightly. Add chicken bouillon cubes and stir in the potatoes, dill, tarragon, thyme, and paprika. Reduce heat to medium, cover, and simmer for 18 to 20 minutes or until potatoes are tender. Remove any skin from the smoked salmon, flake and add to the stockpot. Stir in the lemon juice, hot sauce, salt, pepper, and Half and Half. Simmer over low heat, uncovered, for 10 minutes, stirring occasionally. Do not let the chowder boil after adding the Half and Half. Serve hot.

Suggested Wood Chips For Smoking:
Hickory or Mesquite

You'll Need:

- 8 ounces fresh salmon, cut into ½-inch pieces
- 2 tablespoons butter
- 1 tablespoon extra virgin olive oil
- 1 cup onion, chopped
- 2 cloves garlic, chopped
- ½ cup celery, chopped
- ½ cup all-purpose flour
- 6 ½ cups water
- 2 chicken bouillon cubes
- 1 lb. red potatoes, cubed
- 1 teaspoon dill weed, dried
- 1 teaspoon tarragon, dried
- 1 teaspoon thyme, dried
- ½ teaspoon paprika
- 1 tablespoon fresh lemon juice
- ¼ teaspoon hot sauce
- 1 teaspoon salt
- 1 teaspoon black pepper
- 1 cup Half and Half

SMOKED

JOHN *says*

If your salmon filets do not have the skin, line the cooking racks with aluminum foil before smoking. Also, to make cleanup a breeze, you can line the water bowl and bottom drip tray with aluminum foil. Be sure to make a hole in the bottom drip tray if you line with foil to allow the juices to drain.

Spicy Cuban Smoked Catfish

Serves 7

You'll Need:
- 7 (2 ½ lbs.) catfish filets
- 1 tablespoon paprika
- 1 teaspoon ground cumin
- 1 teaspoon black pepper
- 1 teaspoon salt
- 1 teaspoon onion powder
- ¼ teaspoon cayenne pepper

Sauce:
- ½ cup chicken stock
- ½ cup orange juice
- 2 tablespoons lime juice
- ½ cup vegetable oil

1. In a small bowl, combine the paprika, cumin, pepper, salt, onion powder, and cayenne pepper to make a rub. Reserve 1 tablespoon for mop.

2. Coat catfish filets with rub. Lay filets flat in a large pan, cover and marinate in the refrigerator for at least 3 hours.

3. Load the wood tray with one small handful of wood chips and preheat the smoker to 180° F.

4. In a medium bowl, whisk the chicken stock, orange juice, lime juice, oil, and reserved rub.

5. Smoke the catfish on the top rack of the smoker at 180° F for 1 to 1 ½ hours. Apply marinade with the mop every 20 minutes. The catfish is done when it is flaky and white on the inside.

JOHN *says*

My go-to method for cooking catfish has always involved the fryer. With the smoker, I can experiment with different flavors and enjoy a new twist on an old favorite. Be careful not to marinate the catfish for too long with this recipe, because the lime will "cook" the fish.

Smoked Cabbage

Serves 4

1. Load the wood tray with one small handful of wood chips and preheat the smoker to 225° F.

2. In a small bowl, mix tomatoes, chopped onion, jalapeño, cheese, butter, salt, and pepper. Set aside.

3. Core cabbage, cutting out a good-sized cavity. (Make sure you do not core the base; leave the cabbage open only at one end.) Place the tomato mixture in the cavity and wrap cabbage with heavy-duty aluminum foil. Place cabbage in smoker, cored end up, and smoke for 5 to 6 hours at 225° F.

4. Remove cabbage and discard foil and any blackened leaves. Cut the cabbage into wedges and serve.

You'll Need:

- ½ cup diced tomato, seeded and drained
- 3 tablespoons onion, chopped
- 3 tablespoons jalapeño, chopped
- 4 tablespoons Monterey jack or pepper jack cheese, shredded
- 1 stick unsalted butter, softened
- 1 teaspoon salt
- 1 teaspoon black pepper
- 1 head green or red cabbage

JOHN says

You can use either Savoy or red cabbage for this. Change it up by adding your own combination of ingredients. Be sure to keep the top side up so the butter doesn't run out. You can leave a small opening in the top of the foil to allow for more smoke, but be aware that it's easily overpowered. Decide how much smoke you want, and adjust the opening to suit your taste. This is a great side dish to serve with ribs. Put it in the smoker along with the ribs and they'll both be ready at the same time.

SMOKED

Smoked Trout and Tomato Bruschetta

Serves 8

You'll Need:

- 4 large trout filet pieces, or 1 (1 lb.) whole trout

Marinade:
- 3 cups water
- ¼ cup soy sauce
- ¾ cup teriyaki sauce
- 2 teaspoons salt
- 2 teaspoons lemon pepper
- 1 teaspoon garlic salt
- 1 teaspoon dill weed

Bruschetta:
- 1 loaf French bread, cut into 8 diagonal ½-inch thick slices
- 3 large cloves garlic, halved
- 3 tablespoons extra virgin olive oil
- 1 ¼ lbs. ripe tomatoes, seeded and chopped
- 2 tablespoons fresh parsley, chopped
- 1 tablespoon capers, drained
- ½ teaspoon black pepper
- ½ teaspoon salt
- 1 large avocado
- 1 tablespoon lemon juice, freshly squeezed

Marinade:

1. In a large bowl mix water, soy sauce, teriyaki sauce, salt, lemon pepper, garlic salt, and dill weed. Add filets, cover and refrigerate for 8 hours or overnight.

Smoked Trout:

1. Load the wood tray with one small handful of wood chips and preheat the smoker to 225° F. Smoke trout for 55 minutes, until meat is flaky, or until internal temperature reaches 145° F.

Bruschetta:

1. Place the bread slices about 4-inches from the heat and grill (or broil) for 2 minutes on each side. While still hot, rub bread with garlic and drizzle with oil.

2. In a large bowl, mix tomatoes, parsley, capers, pepper, and salt. Flake the trout with a fork and gently add to tomato mixture.

3. Peel and pit the avocado, then mash. Add lemon juice and mix well. Spread a thin layer of avocado on each slice of bread. Spoon the smoked trout and tomato mixture onto each piece, about ½ cup per slice. Serve immediately.

Suggested Wood For Smoking:

Hickory or Mesquite

JOHN *says*

This appetizer works equally well with trout or mackerel. When selecting your bread for bruschetta, steer clear of lightweight French and Italian loaves with thin crusts and big holes. Look for thick-crusted, dense, French or Italian loaves. When you knock the loaf you should hear a hollow thump.

Smoked Meatloaf

Serves 6 to 8

1. Load the wood tray with one small handful of wood chips and preheat the smoker to 250° F.

2. In a medium skillet, sauté the green peppers, onions, garlic, and olive oil until peppers are soft. Remove from heat and pour into a large mixing bowl. Add ground round, sausage, BBQ sauce, bread crumbs, eggs, salt, pepper, and cayenne pepper, mix thoroughly.

3. Form the meat mixture into four small loaves. Place the loaves into two 11 by 7-inch baking pans lined with foil, 2 small loaves to a pan. Place pans on middle rack and smoke for 2 hours, making sure the internal temperature reaches 160° F.

4. Lightly brush the top of each meatloaf with ketchup 30 minutes before you remove them from the smoker. Allow the meatloaf to rest at least 15 minutes before serving.

Suggested Wood Chips For Smoking:

Hickory or Mesquite

You'll Need:

- 1 ½ cups green pepper, finely chopped
- 2 cups onion, finely chopped
- 1 teaspoon minced garlic
- 1 tablespoon extra virgin olive oil
- 2 lbs. lean ground round
- 1 lb. fresh Italian sausage (removed from casing and crumbled)
- 1 cup BBQ sauce
- 1 cup fresh bread crumbs
- 2 large eggs, lightly beaten
- 1 teaspoon salt
- ½ teaspoon black pepper
- ¼ teaspoon cayenne pepper
- 1 cup ketchup

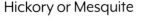

JOHN *says*

Forming the meatloaf mixture into smaller loaves ensures a more even, all-around smoke. Lightly brushing the top of the meatloaf with ketchup gives it an attractive glaze. Make sure you smoke it at 250° F. You need to get your meat to a safe internal temperature of 160° F as quickly as possible.

SMOKED

Smoked Baby Back Ribs
with Espresso BBQ Sauce

Serves 4 to 6

1. Season ribs with salt and pepper and smoke for 3 hours at 225° F, in preheated smoker. Use hickory chips during the first 2 hours.

2. After 3 hours, remove ribs, baste generously with espresso BBQ sauce and wrap in heavy-duty aluminum foil. Return to smoker and cook for an additional 1 to 1 ½ hours, or until internal temperature reaches 160° F.

OPTIONAL: During the last 10 minutes, remove ribs from the foil and baste again; place them back in the smoker, directly onto the rack, allowing the ribs to caramelize. Transfer to cutting board, cut and serve hot.

Espresso BBQ Sauce:

1. In a medium saucepan, combine olive oil and garlic and sauté on medium heat until golden. Remove from heat and let the garlic cool in the oil. Whisk in the ketchup, honey, vinegar, soy sauce, and espresso. Return to heat and simmer for 15 minutes to blend flavors. Remove from heat.

Makes 2 cups

You'll Need:
- 6 lbs. (3 racks) pork baby-back ribs
- Sea salt
- Freshly ground black pepper

Espresso BBQ Sauce:
- 2 tablespoons extra virgin olive oil
- 2 tablespoons minced garlic
- 1 cup ketchup
- 1 cup honey
- ½ cup balsamic vinegar
- ¼ cup soy sauce
- ¼ cup Starbucks® double shot espresso, or strong homebrewed coffee

Smoked Corn on the Cob
with Potatoes

Serves 4 to 6

Corn:

1. Load the wood tray with one small handful of wood chips and preheat the smoker to 225° F.

2. Prepare corn by gently pulling back the husks on each ear. Remove the silk, but not the husks. Place the ears in a large pan and fill with water to cover corn. Let soak for 2 hours.

3. Remove corn from water and pat dry with paper towels. Pull husk back to reveal corn, brush each ear with olive oil and sprinkle with 1 to 2 teaspoons of green onions, salt, and pepper. Pull husks back over corn and place in a 225° F smoker for about 1 ½ hours. Serve with or without husks, but remove husks to eat.

Potatoes:

1. Wash and slice potatoes into ½-inch slices. Place on aluminum foil. Lightly season with olive oil and garlic salt (or use your favorite herbs and spices). Place foil on rack in smoker and cook potatoes for the last 45 minutes of smoking time for the corn. Remove from smoker and serve.

You'll Need:

Corn:
- 6 to 12 ears corn with husk on
- ½ cup olive oil
- 1 bunch green onions, finely chopped
- $\frac{1}{16}$ teaspoon salt
- $\frac{1}{16}$ teaspoon pepper

Potatoes:
- 4 to 6 Idaho potatoes (baking)
- 1 tablespoon olive oil
- 1 teaspoon garlic salt

Suggested Wood Chips For Smoking:
Hickory

SMOKED

Smoked Turkey Burgers

Serves 4 to 6

1. Load the wood tray with one small handful of wood chips and preheat the smoker to 225° F.

2. In a large bowl, mix ground turkey, Heinz 57 Sauce, and A-1 Steak Sauce. Mix well. Form patty mixture to desired thickness and shape. Sprinkle lightly with garlic powder, salt, and pepper.

3. Place turkey burgers on bottom rack of smoker and smoke for approximately 30 minutes. Flip and smoke for 30 minutes more, or until internal temperature reaches 165° F.

Suggested Wood Chips For Smoking:

Hickory or Mesquite

You'll Need:

- 3 lbs. ground turkey
- ½ cup Heinz 57 Sauce
- ¼ cup A1 Steak Sauce
- ¼ teaspoon garlic powder
- 1/16 teaspoon salt
- 1/16 teaspoon black pepper

JOHN *says*

If you want to make life simple you can buy pre-made turkey burgers and add the sauce before smoking. When you reduce fat by cooking turkey burgers, you don't have to sacrifice flavor. Add a tablespoon of Worcestershire sauce or your favorite steak sauce to your mix and you won't miss a thing.

SMOKED

Duck Salad
with Citrus Dressing
Serves 6

You'll Need:
- 1 duck breast, skin on

Dressing:
- ⅓ cup orange juice
- 3 tablespoons fresh lemon juice
- 2 tablespoons rice wine vinegar
- 1 tablespoon sugar
- 2 tablespoons sesame oil
- 1 tablespoon fresh chives, chopped
- ½ teaspoon kosher salt
- ¼ teaspoon black pepper
- 1 (5 ounce) bag fresh mixed lettuce

1. Load the wood tray with one small handful of wood chips and preheat the smoker to 225° F.

2. Prepare the duck by pouring boiling water over the skin to render some of the fat. Place duck in the smoker and cook at 225° F for 1 hour per pound. Smoke until duck breast reaches an internal temperature of 165° F. Remove from smoker and slice into thin strips.

Sauce:

1. In a medium bowl, mix orange juice, lemon juice, vinegar, sugar, sesame oil, chives, salt, and pepper. Add to a dressing bottle or suitable container and shake.

2. Place lettuce on serving plates and top with sliced duck. Drizzle dressing over the salad and serve.

JOHN *says*

Duck is a fatty bird (unless you've just shot a wild duck), so part of the challenge with any recipe is to cut the fat off or find ways of letting the fat drain during the cooking process. If you're cooking the breast or the whole bird, you'll need to score the skin of the duck. When scoring the skin, lightly cut the surface and into the fat. Don't cut down into the meat, or you'll end up with a dry bird.

Smoked Salmon Dip

Serves 4

1. Load the wood tray with one small handful of wood chips and preheat the smoker to 225° F.

2. Lay salmon steaks flat and season them with lemon juice, olive oil, parsley flakes, and Butterball® Cajun Seasoning.

3. Place salmon on the middle rack and smoke for 1 to 2 hours, or until internal temperature reaches 145° F. Remove salmon from smoker and let cool.

4. In a large bowl, combine mustard, green onions, pecans, dressing, grapes, and mayonnaise. Crumble salmon steaks into mixture and stir until well mixed. Chill and serve with bagel chips.

Suggested Wood Chips For Smoking:

Apple or Mesquite

You'll Need:

- 4 to 6 salmon steaks
- ½ lemon, juiced
- 1 tablespoon extra virgin olive oil
- 1 tablespoon parsley flakes
- 1 tablespoon Butterball Cajun Seasoning
- 3 tablespoons Creole mustard
- 2 bunches green onions, sliced
- 1 cup chopped pecans
- ½ cup Greek dressing
- 1 small bunch seedless red grapes, halved
- Hellmann's mayonnaise
- Bagel chips

JOHN *says*

Smoking salmon creates an incredible flavor and allows spices to infuse throughout the fish. Check doneness during the first hour of cooking and don't overcook; fish will dry out. Fish flakes with a fork when done. Not only will you love this Smoked Salmon Dip, it ain't bad served as an entrée either.

SMOKED

Smoked Steaks
with BBQ Glaze
Serves 4

1. Rub the steaks with garlic, pepper, and 2 ½ teaspoons salt. Place in a large pan and pour pomegranate juice onto steaks. Cover and marinate in the refrigerator for several hours. Remove and allow to warm to room temperature before you remove steaks from marinade.

2. Load the wood tray with one small handful of wood chips and preheat the smoker to 225° F. Place steaks on top rack of smoker and cook at 225° F for at least 1 hour (for medium), 1 ½ hours (for medium well), or 2 hours (for well done). Brush with glaze during cooking. Serve with reserved glaze.

3. Cream together butter, ½ teaspoon salt, and basil in a bowl or food processor. Dot the steaks with herb butter and salt before serving.

BBQ Glaze:

1. Heat oil on medium heat in a saucepan and sauté onion and garlic until soft about 5 minutes. Add vinegar, pomegranate juice, ketchup, Worcestershire sauce, brown sugar, chili powder, molasses, oregano, thyme, paprika, and hot sauce. Bring to a boil. Lower heat and simmer uncovered for 20 minutes. Brush glaze over steaks while cooking.

Suggested Wood Chips For Smoking:
Hickory or Mesquite

You'll Need:
- 4 (1-inch thick) medium ribeyes or T-bone steaks
- 3 cloves garlic, minced
- 2 teaspoons black pepper
- 3 teaspoons kosher salt
- ¼ cup pomegranate juice
- ¼ cup unsalted butter
- ¼ cup fresh basil leaves, chopped

BBQ Glaze:
- 1 tablespoon olive oil
- ½ red onion, chopped
- 5 cloves garlic, minced
- 2 tablespoons cider vinegar
- 2 cups pomegranate juice
- 1 ½ cups ketchup
- 3 tablespoons Worcestershire sauce
- 3 tablespoons dark brown sugar
- 2 tablespoons chili powder
- 2 tablespoons molasses
- 1 tablespoon dried oregano
- 1 tablespoon dried thyme
- 1 tablespoon paprika
- 1 teaspoon hot sauce (Tabasco style)

JOHN *says*

Smoking a ribeye allows you to break away from traditional grilled steak, and it has great flavor. The thickness of the steak determines your cooking time. My wife likes thinner steaks (about ½-inch), so I simply cut the smoking time in half.

Tandoori Chicken

Serves 2 to 4

1. In a large bowl, mix the salt, garlic, lemon juice, yogurt, turmeric, garam masala, cayenne pepper, and food coloring. Add chicken to the marinade, cover, and refrigerate for at least 4 hours.

2. Load the wood tray with one small handful of wood chips and preheat the smoker to 225° F. Remove chicken from the marinade and place on rack inside smoker. Smoke for 1 to 1 ½ hours or until thickest part of the meat reaches an internal temperature of 165° F. In the last ½ hour of cooking time, brush oil on the chicken several times while grilling.

You'll Need:

- 1 teaspoon salt
- 3 cloves garlic, minced
- 2 tablespoons lemon juice
- 1 cup plain yogurt
- ½ teaspoon turmeric
- 2 teaspoons garam masala (an Indian spice found in most grocery stores)
- ½ teaspoon cayenne pepper
- ¼ teaspoon orange food coloring
- 8 chicken thighs, skin removed
- 2 teaspoons olive oil, for brushing

JOHN says

This unique dish takes its name from *Tandoor*, a traditional Indian clay oven. Technically, anything cooked in it and marinated in this manner assumes the name, *Tandoori*. You can also grill this recipe in about half the time and either method is bone-suckin' *Dadgum Good.*

SMOKED

Butterflied Leg of Lamb
with Honey and Herb Sauce
Serves 4 to 6

1. Load the wood tray with one small handful of wood chips and preheat the smoker to 225° F.

2. Trim fat from the meat. Lay the lamb out flat, and score with a knife crosswise, several times on both sides. Mix the oil, garlic, rosemary, thyme, parsley, salt, and pepper, and rub into both sides of the lamb. Roll lamb, starting from the shortest end. Using butcher's twine, wrap the lamb roast and tie the ends.

3. Place lamb in smoker, seam side down, and smoke for 2 ½ hours, or until meat reaches an internal temperature of 150° F.

4. Remove lamb from smoker and drizzle with lemon juice. Cover with aluminum foil and let rest for 10 minutes. The temperature of the meat after standing should be 145° F for medium rare, and 160° F for medium doneness.

Honey and Herb Sauce:

1. Mix the jelly, honey, orange juice, vinegar, and cayenne pepper in a small saucepan. Heat gently until all ingredients are combined. Drizzle the sauce over the freshly sliced lamb.

You'll Need:
- 1 (4 ½ lb.) leg of lamb, butterflied
- ¼ cup olive oil
- 6 cloves garlic, minced
- 2 tablespoons fresh rosemary, chopped
- 2 tablespoons fresh thyme, chopped
- 2 tablespoons fresh parsley, chopped
- 1 teaspoon salt
- 1 teaspoon black pepper
- 2 tablespoons fresh lemon juice

Honey and Herb Sauce:
- ⅓ cup red currant jelly
- 2 tablespoons honey
- 2 tablespoons orange juice
- 1 tablespoon apple cider vinegar
- ¼ teaspoon cayenne pepper

SMOKED

JOHN says

When selecting a leg of lamb for this dish, ask your butcher to butterfly it for you. By butterflying a leg of lamb, you get a thinner piece of meat which will shorten the required cooking time. You also increase the effectiveness of a marinade or dry rub since there will be more meat surface to absorb the *Dadgum Good* flavors.

Moroccan Ground Beef Kabobs

Serves 2

1. Load the wood tray with one small handful of wood chips and preheat the smoker to 225° F.

2. Soak skewers in water for 10 minutes. Combine ground beef, parsley, mint, cumin, coriander, garlic, paprika, turmeric, cinnamon, onion, and egg in large mixing bowl; mix until thoroughly combined. Form meat mixture into 1-inch balls and thread onto wooden skewers.

3. Place skewer directly on smoker racks and cook at 225° F for 45 minutes, or until internal temperature reaches 160° F.

Suggested Wood Chips For Smoking:
Mesquite

You'll Need:
- Skewers, soaked in water to moisten
- 1 ½ lbs. lean ground beef
- ¼ cup fresh parsley, chopped
- ¼ tablespoon fresh mint, chopped
- 2 teaspoons ground cumin
- 2 teaspoons ground coriander
- 2 cloves garlic, minced
- 2 teaspoons paprika
- ½ teaspoon turmeric
- ½ teaspoon cinnamon
- 1 small onion, finely chopped
- 1 egg

JOHN *says*

This is a dish that has probably been around since the invention of fire. You can try it in true Moroccan-style and use ground lamb, but beef works just fine. The secret is to make sure the meat is sticky enough to hold together on the skewers. Once it starts cooking, the meat will firm up and hold.

Smoked Pork Loin
with Mustard, Apricot, and Brown Sugar Glaze
Serves 6 to 8

1. In a large bowl, stir together water, salt, and sugar. Submerge pork and refrigerate overnight for 8 to 12 hours. Remove from refrigerator, drain and tie with several pieces of butcher twine to help hold shape. Score the fat, if thick, but do not cut into the meat.

2. Load the wood tray with one small handful of wood chips and preheat the smoker to 250° F. Reduce to 225° F to smoke and continue adding wood chips every hour during cooking.

3. To make the glaze, combine the Dijon, apricot preserves, brown sugar, garlic, salt, and pepper in a small bowl. Rub the mixture all over the meat, reserving ⅓ cup. Place the pork loin in the smoker on middle rack and smoke for 3 ½ hours at 225° F, or until internal temperature reaches 165° F.

4. Remove from smoker, wrap in aluminum foil and continue smoking for another 1 ½ hours, until the meat thermometer reads 165° F (no more wood chips are necessary). Remove from smoker and allow to rest covered in foil for an additional 30 minutes. Heat the reserved rub mixture in the microwave on high until warm and serve with sliced warm pork.

You'll Need:
- 4 quarts cool water
- 2 cups kosher salt
- 2 cups sugar
- 1 (4 to 5 lb.) pork loin, untrimmed

Glaze:
- ½ cup good whole grain Dijon mustard
- ½ cup apricot preserves
- 2 tablespoons brown sugar
- 2 cloves garlic, minced
- 1 teaspoon salt
- 1 teaspoon black pepper

JOHN *says*

Take care not to overcook this delicate, lean meat. Remove the loin from the smoker when the internal temperature reaches about 165° F. Above 165° F the loin will start to dry out. If this happens, the glaze comes in handy.

SMOKED

Salmon Steaks
with
Citrus Salsa
Serves 4

You'll Need:

- 1 teaspoon sea salt
- 1 teaspoon black pepper
- ½ lemon, juiced
- 2 limes, juiced
- 1 tablespoon fresh basil, chopped
- 1 tablespoon light brown sugar
- 4 salmon steaks, boned

Citrus Salsa:

- 3 cups papaya, peeled and diced
- 2 cups fresh pineapple, diced
- ½ cup green onion, chopped
- 1 cup ripe mango, chopped
- 2 tablespoons cilantro, chopped
- 2 tablespoons lime juice
- ½ teaspoon salt
- 1 tablespoon sugar

1. In a small bowl, combine salt, pepper, lemon juice, lime juice (reserving 2 tablespoons for the Salsa), basil, and brown sugar. Place the salmon in a large bowl, cover with marinade over and refrigerate for a minimum of 30 to 45 minutes.

2. Load the wood tray with one small handful of wood chips and preheat the smoker to 225° F. Place salmon on middle smoker rack and smoke for 45 minutes to 1 hour, brushing occasionally with any leftover marinade. Add more wood chips about every 30 minutes.

3. Serve topped with citrus salsa.

Citrus Salsa:

1. In a medium bowl, combine papaya, pineapple, green onions, mango, cilantro, lime juice, salt, and sugar, mixing well.

JOHN *says*

To enhance the succulence and flavor of this dish, consider brining the salmon first in a simple solution of 2 quarts water, ½ cup kosher salt and ½ cup brown sugar. It will improve the moisture content and even enhance the color of the salmon. This recipe can also be grilled and only takes half the cooking time.

Smoked BBQ Shrimp

Serves 4 to 6

1. Load the wood tray with a small handful of wood chips and preheat the smoker to 225° F.

2. In a medium-size bowl, mix together melted butter, dressing, pepper, garlic powder, Worcestershire sauce, and Butterball® Cajun Seasoning. Place washed and drained shrimp with shells-on in a large disposable aluminum pan and cover with the liquid mixture.

3. Place pan of shrimp on middle rack of smoker and cook, uncovered for 1 ½ hours or until internal temperature reaches 145° F. Stir the shrimp halfway through the smoking process. Serve with French bread for dipping in the shrimp sauce.

You'll Need:

- 2 sticks butter, melted
- 12 ounces (½ bottle) Italian dressing
- 1 tablespoon black pepper
- 2 teaspoons garlic powder
- ½ cup Worcestershire sauce
- ½ teaspoon Butterball Cajun Seasoning
- 5 lbs. medium raw shrimp (shell-on)

JOHN says

Bring the bayou to your backyard with this smoked shrimp recipe. You can add the shrimp to a salad or make a non-fried Po' Boy sandwich for a healthy alternative. Stirring the shrimp halfway through the smoking process evenly distributes the flavors.

SMOKED

Smoked Beef Brisket

Serves 6 to 8

You'll Need:

Marinade:

- 3 cups beef stock
- ¾ cup Worcestershire sauce
- ½ cup ketchup
- ½ cup fresh lemon juice
- 2 tablespoons yellow mustard
- 1 tablespoon Asian chili paste
- 1 tablespoon chili powder
- 1 teaspoon celery seed, ground
- 2 teaspoons seasoning salt
- 1 teaspoon cumin
- 1 teaspoon granulated onion

Rub:

- 1 ¼ cups light brown sugar
- ½ cup kosher salt
- ¼ cup garlic salt
- ¼ cup seasoning salt
- ¼ cup granulated onion
- ¼ cup unseasoned chili powder
- ¼ cup paprika
- ¼ cup black pepper
- 2 tablespoons lemon pepper
- 2 tablespoons cayenne pepper

Brisket:

- 1 (6 to 10 lb.) beef brisket

Sauce:

- 1 medium onion, peeled and quartered
- ¼ cup water
- 1 cup ketchup
- 2 tablespoons cider vinegar
- 2 tablespoons Worcestershire sauce
- 2 tablespoons Dijon mustard
- 5 tablespoons molasses
- 1 teaspoon hot pepper sauce
- 2 tablespoons vegetable oil
- 1 teaspoon minced garlic
- 1 teaspoon chili powder
- ¼ teaspoon cayenne pepper

Marinade:

1. In a large saucepan, combine all marinade ingredients and bring to a boil. Reduce heat and simmer for 10 minutes. Set aside to cool.

2. Marinate brisket for 4 to 6 hours in the refrigerator. Remove brisket from marinade, dry with paper towels, and let it sit for ½ hour. Reserve marinade for basting during smoking.

3. Trim excess brisket fat, leaving to a ½-inch layer. Be careful not to cut into the meat.

Rub:

1. In a medium-size bowl, combine all rub ingredients, and apply the rub to brisket just before placing in the smoker.

Brisket:

1. Load the wood tray with one small handful of wood chips and preheat the smoker to 250° F. Reduce heat to 225° F, then add the brisket.

2. Place the brisket in the smoker and cook at 225°F for 4 hours, until a bark begins to form. Apply marinade every hour to prevent the brisket from drying out. Continue to smoke the brisket until the internal temperature reaches 165° F. (Total smoking time is approximately 60 minutes per pound.)

3. After 4 hours, remove the brisket, wrap in aluminum foil, and continue cooking an additional 3 to 4 hours until the temperature reaches 195° F. Remove from smoker and let stand for 15 minutes in foil before carving.

Sauce:

1. Pulse onion and ¼ cup water in food processor for 30 seconds. Strain mixture to obtain ½ cup juice. Discard solids left in strainer.

2. In a medium bowl, whisk together the onion juice, ketchup, vinegar, Worcestershire, mustard, molasses, and hot pepper sauce. Set aside.

3. In a large saucepan, heat oil over medium heat until shimmering but not smoking. Add garlic, chili powder, and cayenne pepper; cook for 30 seconds. Whisk in ketchup mixture and bring to boil. Reduce heat to medium-low and simmer gently, uncovered until sauce is thickened, about 25 minutes. Cool sauce to room temperature before using.

JOHN says

Making a great beef brisket starts with choosing a great cut of meat. You're going to want a brisket that's well-marbled, but make sure it's not too fatty on the outside. Look for a ½-inch layer of fat on the top. That'll help produce a moist, tender outcome.

To tell whether you've bought a good piece of brisket, pick it up and hold it in the middle. It should be flexible. If the brisket is stiff, you're starting on the back foot. Bigger could equal tougher, and remember you'll be slow smoking it for 1 hour per pound at 225° F.

Serve with the sauce on the side. Some say a good brisket needs no sauce.

SMOKED

Smoked Onion Burgers

Serves 8 to 10

You'll Need:

- 2 lbs. ground chuck, extra lean
- 1 lb. ground beef
- 1 package onion soup mix

1. Load the wood tray with one small handful of wood chips and preheat the smoker to 275° F.

2. In a large bowl, combine the ground chuck, ground beef, and onion soup mix. Form meat mixture into patties about ½-inch thick. (You should get 8 to 10 burgers.)

3. Reduce smoker heat to 225° F. Place hamburgers on middle rack and smoke for 1 hour. Flip hamburgers and smoke for an additional 30 minutes to 1 hour, or until desired doneness is reached.

Suggested Wood Chips For Smoking:
Hickory

JOHN says

Getting a smoked burger right can be a tough balancing act. You don't want to undercook it or dry it out. To get a juicy-tasting burger, use meat that's 80% lean. You can also add a tablespoon of beef stock or tomato sauce to your patty mix. For safety's sake, turn your smoker up to 275° F before you start smoking. Bring it back down to 225° F when you put the burgers in, and then remember to use a meat thermometer to test for doneness. Your burgers will be ready when the internal temperature reaches 160° F.

Fish Jambalaya

Serves 4 to 6

1. Load the wood tray with one small handful of wood chips and preheat the smoker to 225° F. Place the fish on the top rack of the smoker and cook for 45 minutes, or until internal temperature reaches 145° F.

2. While fish is in smoker, lightly brown the onions in butter and oil in a large frying pan. Add the potatoes and fry until golden brown. Stir in the jalapeños, ginger, tomato, and vegetable stock. Cook over a low heat for 5 minutes. Cook rice according to package instructions.

3. Remove smoked fish from smoker and flake, then add to frying pan. Add rice and yellow raisins, spoon mixture to serving plates and season with lemon juice, salt, and pepper.

You'll Need:

- 4 fish filets, boned and skinned (preferably Amberjack, or your favorite fish)
- 2 medium yellow onions, finely sliced
- 2 tablespoons butter, unsalted
- 2 tablespoons extra virgin olive oil
- 3 large red potatoes (2 cups), peeled and cubed
- 2 jalapeños, seeded and finely chopped
- 1 teaspoon fresh ginger, finely chopped
- 1 (14 ounce) can diced tomatoes
- ¾ cup vegetable stock
- 2 cups cooked white rice
- 4 tablespoons yellow raisins
- 3 tablespoons freshly squeezed lemon juice
- 1 teaspoon kosher salt
- 1 teaspoon black pepper

SMOKED

JOHN *says*

For those who are unsure if they want rice or potatoes for dinner, this dish gives you the best of both worlds. With all of those carbs, the fish helps you not feel so guilty after the meal. Don't forget to coat the smoker racks with non-stick spray before adding the fish.

Mustard Glazed Smoked Ham

Serves 10 to 12

1. Place the ham in a large pot and cover with cold water. Add onion, carrots, bay leaves, allspice and peppercorns. Bring to a boil, then reduce heat, cover and gently simmer for 20 minutes.

2. Remove ham and place in a roasting pan to cool. Discard marinade. Once cooled, use a sharp knife to score the ham in a diamond pattern.

Mustard Glaze:

1. In a small mixing bowl, combine apricot preserves, Dijon mustard, mustard powder, whole grain mustard, and orange juice.

2. Brush mustard glaze on ham, covering it completely. Let ham stand in glaze for 1 to 2 hours, basting frequently at room temperature before smoking.

3. Load the wood tray with one small handful of wood chips and preheat the smoker to 225° F.

4. Place ham in smoker and cook for 2 to 3 hours, or until the internal temperature reaches 160° F. Baste at least 2 more times during the smoking process.

Suggested Wood Chips For Smoking:

Hickory or Mesquite

You'll Need:

- 1 (5 to 7 lb.) fully-cooked ham, bone in
- 1 onion, quartered
- 2 carrots, quartered
- 3 bay leaves
- 1 tablespoon ground allspice
- 1 teaspoon black peppercorns

Mustard Glaze:

- 1 cup smooth apricot preserve
- 2 tablespoons Dijon mustard
- 2 teaspoons English or Canadian mustard powder
- 4 tablespoons whole grain mustard
- 4 tablespoons orange juice

SMOKED

JOHN *says*

Hams are sold bone-in and boneless. I recommend smoking the ham with the bone in. It produces a better texture and taste. When testing for doneness, make sure you use a meat thermometer and be careful not to touch the bone, which may give you a false temperature reading.

BBQ Venison

Serves 4 to 8

1. In medium bowl, combine tomato sauce, smoked BBQ sauce, Worcestershire sauce, honey, onion, lemon juice, garlic, chicken bouillon, brown sugar, chili powder, red grape juice, and water. Marinate venison for 8 to 12 hours in refrigerator. Reserve ⅓ of marinade for basting venison while smoking.

2. Preheat the smoker to 180° F. Remove the venison from the marinade and wrap the bacon slices around the roast, securing them with toothpicks. Place roast in smoker and smoke for 4 to 6 hours or until the internal temperature reaches 145° F.

3. In a saucepan, bring the marinade to a boil. Reduce heat and cover to simmer. Brush the roast with the reserved marinade during the smoking process.

JOHN says

Venison tastes great, but some don't enjoy its gamey flavor. It's also lean and without the right preparation it can come out drier than the Sahara desert. Here's a recipe that solves both problems. You can also soak the roast in buttermilk for an hour to draw out the wild taste prior to marinating. When you're smoking venison, use prime cuts such as top round, sirloin tip, back strap and rump roasts. These cuts are naturally tender. The right marinade will eliminate the gamey taste and the bacon wrap around the roast eliminates the need for constant basting. Don't overcook the venison. Remove it from the smoker about 5° F before it reaches its target temperature of 145° F. Internal temperature will continue to increase for about 10 minutes.

You'll Need:
- ½ cup tomato sauce
- ½ cup smoked BBQ sauce
- 2 tablespoons Worcestershire sauce
- 1 tablespoon honey
- 1 small onion, finely chopped
- 1 teaspoon lemon or lime juice
- 1 clove garlic, minced
- 1 chicken bouillon cube, crumbled
- 1 tablespoon brown sugar
- ½ teaspoon chilli powder
- ¼ cup red grape juice
- ¼ cup water
- 1 (2 to 4 lb.) venison roast
- 6 slices of bacon

Orange Chicken
with Marmalade Butter
Serves 4 to 6

1. To make a marinade, mix together orange juice, garlic, salt, pepper, and oil in a large bowl. Add chicken thighs and marinate in refrigerator for at least 4 hours.

2. Load the wood tray with one small handful of wood chips and preheat the smoker to 225° F. Remove chicken from marinade and place on middle rack and smoke for approximately 1 ½ hours or until internal temperature reaches 165° F.

3. Reduce smoker temperature to 225° F and add more wood chips every 30 minutes.

4. In a small saucepan, bring marinade mixture to a boil. Baste chicken with warm marinade while cooking.

Marmalade Butter:

1. In a small bowl, combine butter, orange, cilantro, shallot, orange marmalade, and salt. Cream together and chill. Serve with hot, smoked chicken.

You'll Need:
- 1 cup freshly squeezed orange juice
- 1 clove garlic, minced
- 1 teaspoon kosher salt
- ½ teaspoon black pepper
- 2 tablespoons sesame oil
- 8 chicken thighs

Marmalade Butter:
- ½ cup unsalted butter, softened
- 1 tablespoon orange rind, grated and chopped
- 1 tablespoon cilantro, chopped
- 1 shallot, finely chopped
- 2 tablespoons orange marmalade
- 1 teaspoon kosher salt

SMOKED

JOHN *says*

For the best outcome, choose thighs with the bone in. The bone reduces the shrinkage of the meat during smoking. It also helps to retain moisture and adds flavor. You can use a meat thermometer to test for doneness or pull meat away from the bone to check. When the internal temperature reaches 165° F, you're good to go.

Smoked Potato and Green Chili Casserole

Serves 4 to 6

1. Load the wood tray with one small handful of wood chips and preheat the smoker to 200° F.

2. Cut the potatoes into 1-inch thick slices and lightly coat with vegetable oil. Place the potatoes and Poblano peppers on a sheet of heavy-duty aluminum foil and place on rack of smoker for 1 hour until partially cooked. Cool the potatoes and slice again to ¼-inch thickness.

3. Preheat oven to 350° F. In a small bowl, mix the chiles, cheese, and onion. Set aside for layering.

4. Layer ½ of the potatoes in a greased casserole dish. On top of the potatoes, spread ½ of the cheese and chili mixture. Top with ½ cup whipping cream and sprinkle with salt and pepper. Repeat this process until all ingredients are used.

5. Bake casserole in oven for 20 minutes.

Suggested Wood Chips For Smoking:
Hickory

You'll Need:

- 3 medium Idaho potatoes
- Vegetable oil for coating
- ¾ cup Poblano chiles, chopped
- 1 ½ cups pepper jack cheese, shredded
- ⅓ cup red onion, finely chopped
- 1 cup whipping cream
- Salt and black pepper

JOHN *says*

We Southerners love our potatoes in casseroles, salads, baked, boiled, mashed... you name it! This recipe is a great way to marry a Southern dish with the flavors of Mexico. I'm not a big fan of red onions, so I tone my casserole down by using a milder version, such as a sweet Vidalia or yellow onion.

Country Sausage

Serves 4 to 6

1. In a large bowl, combine ground chuck, pork, bacon, garlic, Worcestershire sauce, coriander, cloves, nutmeg, cayenne pepper, salt, and pepper. Form the mixture into a roll, 2 ½-inches thick. Wrap in plastic cling wrap and twist the two ends tightly to create a seal. Refrigerate for 1 hour.

2. Load the wood tray with one small handful of wood chips and preheat the smoker to 225° F.

3. Remove sausage from wrapping and place directly on smoker rack. Place a disposable aluminum pan on the rack directly underneath the sausage to catch the fat drippings. Smoke the sausage for 2 hours, or until internal temperature is 165° F. Slice to serve.

Suggested Wood Chips For Smoking:

Hickory or Mesquite

JOHN *says*

If you don't want to go through the tedium of stuffing a sausage, this skinless sausage recipe is a convenient alternative. It will drip fat, so make sure you place it directly over the smoker's water pan, or place a disposable aluminum pan on the rack directly underneath the sausage as it cooks.

You'll Need:
- 2 lbs. ground chuck
- 1 lb. ground pork
- ½ lb. raw bacon, finely chopped
- 2 cloves garlic, minced
- 2 tablespoons Worcestershire sauce
- 1 tablespoon ground coriander
- 1 teaspoon ground cloves
- ½ teaspoon ground nutmeg
- 1 teaspoon cayenne pepper
- 1 tablespoon salt
- 1 teaspoon black pepper

Salmon and Avocado Salad

Serves 4

1. Load the wood tray with one small handful of wood chips and preheat the smoker to 250° F.

2. Reduce smoker temperature to 225° F and place salmon directly on rack. Smoke for 40 minutes or until internal temperature reaches 145° F. While salmon is in smoker, gently mix the tomato, avocado, onion, dill, salt, pepper, cayenne pepper and ½ of the lemon juice (reserve the other ½ for the dressing) in a medium bowl. When salmon is cooked, remove any skin from fish; flake, and add to the avocado mixture. Then place the mixture in 4 small ramekins, pack firmly and set aside. Prepare the dressing by mixing the remaining lemon juice, olive oil, and a pinch of black pepper.

3. Place the salad greens on 4 small plates and lightly coat with the dressing. Upend one ramekin on the bed of greens to remove the salmon mixture and garnish with cherry tomatoes and dill. Repeat process for the remaining 3 plates. Add a squeeze of lemon juice to each salad and serve.

You'll Need:

- 8 (8 ounce) salmon steaks, smoked and flaked
- 1 large ripe tomato, chopped
- 1 avocado, diced
- ¼ cup onion, chopped
- 1 tablespoon dill, finely chopped
- 1 large lemon, cut in half
- Salt and black pepper
- 1/16 teaspoon of cayenne
- 1 tablespoon olive oil
- 12 ounces (¾ lb.) of mixed salad greens
- 32 cherry tomatoes

Suggested Wood Chips For Smoking:
Hickory

JOHN *says*

I had to look up the word "ramekin" to discover it was a small dish. Go figure! On a more serious note, be sure to select your avocados carefully. I've learned that color isn't always a reliable indicator, so apply the squeeze test instead. A ripe avocado is relatively firm, but will yield to gentle pressure when held in the palm of the hand and squeezed. If you plan to use avocados immediately, buy ripe ones. If you buy them a few days before you use them, buy firm avocados that don't yield to squeezing. Set them out in a cool place to ripen.

SMOKED

Smoked Shrimp and Cream Cheese Spread

Serves 4

1. Load the wood tray with one small handful of wood chips and preheat the smoker to 225° F.

2. Place shrimp in medium-sized metal pan and smoke for 30 minutes at 225° F, until shrimp turns pink. Remove shrimp from smoker and finely chop.

3. In a large mixing bowl, combine cream cheese, chopped green onions, lemon juice, dill, salt, and pepper. Mix well and add chopped shrimp. Top with chopped black olives and serve with fresh country bread or bagel chips.

JOHN *says*

To get a smooth texture in your dip, use the whipped cream cheese sold in tubs, not the regular cream cheese in blocks. I'm sure most folks would eat this dip on fancy little bread. Honestly, for me, it's straight out of the mixing bowl with Frito Scoops. This may irritate most wives, but mine loves to eat it this way! (Which makes me love her even more!)

You'll Need:
- 1 lb. shrimp, peeled and deveined
- 1 (12 ounce) package soft cream cheese
- 6 chopped green onions
- 1 large lemon, juiced
- 3 to 4 tablespoons fresh dill, finely chopped
- Salt and black pepper
- Black olives, chopped for garnish

Smoked Pork Tenderloins

Serves 4 to 8

1. In a small bowl, combine the garlic, cinnamon, ginger, brown sugar, and soy sauce. Rub mixture over tenderloins, cover and marinate for at least 2 hours in refrigerator.

2. Load the wood tray with one small handful of wood chips and preheat the smoker to 225° F. Place tenderloins in smoker on middle rack and smoke for 1 ½ hours or until the internal temperature is 160° F.

Sauce:

1. In a small saucepan, combine garlic, soy sauce, vinegar, honey, Asian hot sauce, cilantro, ginger, peanut butter, orange juice, and brown sugar, simmering for 5 minutes until thickened. Drizzle over tenderloin slices.

You'll Need:

- 3 cloves garlic, crushed
- 1 teaspoon cinnamon
- 1 tablespoon fresh ginger, minced
- 1 tablespoon dark brown sugar
- 2 tablespoons soy sauce
- 2 (1 lb.) pork tenderloins

Sauce:

- 2 cloves garlic, minced
- ⅓ cup soy sauce
- 1 tablespoon rice vinegar
- 2 tablespoons honey
- 1 teaspoon Asian hot sauce (preferably Sriracha)
- 1 tablespoon cilantro, minced
- 1 teaspoon fresh ginger, minced
- 3 tablespoons creamy peanut butter
- ⅓ cup orange juice
- 1 tablespoon brown sugar

JOHN *says*

You're thinking "peanut butter?" Yes, peanut butter! It adds a deliciously nutty flavor that complements the pork. Have a little fun – not all pork has to be served with BBQ sauce.

The Masterbuilt Story
as told by John McLemore

Now we faced the task of telling the world about a product that was (and still is) truly a breakthrough for deep frying turkeys. We'd seen all sorts of products sold by pitchmen on television—each making outrageous claims about their originality, indispensability and the power to simplify your entire life.

It was only natural that in 2003, the folks at QVC would greet the world's first indoor electric fryer with a healthy dose of skepticism. They agreed to dip their toe in the water, and allowed us to promote 1,600 units. Eight minutes into our first airing, we had sold every turkey fryer. It was one of the No. 1 products of the show and QVC knew they had a hit on their hands.

As our company began to enjoy national success, Don and I found ourselves torn between our growing business duties and our desire to enjoy time with our families. We missed the get-togethers and the family dinners that kept us close. Oddly enough, this tension served as motivation for our next product innovation, our Masterbuilt Electric Smoker.

Don and I loved the ritual of smoking foods, but we did not have all day to watch over a smoker and monitor it minute-by-minute. We knew that "low and slow" was the way to go, but our busy lives demanded a convenient, hassle-free and less intimidating smoker for all to enjoy—a digital smoker that was so simple to use it would give the average cook the bragging rights of a professional pit master.

All the sweat that went into our turkey fryer seemed to pay off in developing our digital smoker. But if the smoker design came easily, the same couldn't be said for our efforts to cook the perfect brisket. Now, that's a smoking recipe that certainly separates the men from the boys, and we're happy to say—several dozen briskets later—we've found a recipe you're going to love (see page 142.)

Top:
John's children enjoy a day at QVC with Dad

Bottom Left:
John and Don at Live John Boy and Billy Radio Show

Bottom Center:
Don with son, Blake and John's daughter, Brooke

Bottom Right:
Don, Rick Burgess, and John chowed down on ribs at the Rick & Bubba Show

With our fryers and smokers, we had clearly identified a niche for people who valued convenience and simplicity. With this in mind, Don and I created the Veranda Grill. Tonya and Lynne both found grilling intimidating. They didn't like the idea of cooking with gas or messing with charcoal. Besides, to them, grilling was a "guy thing."

We set about solving this problem with the Veranda Grill, so that it would reduce grilling to a process so simple, anyone could get great results, anywhere. Even on an apartment porch or a condo balcony.

According to Tonya, her first experience with the Electric Veranda went something like this:

"We had a dinner party planned and John, who usually does all the grilling, was supposed to fire up the grill before the guests arrived. I guess time got away from us and John asked me to pop dinner on the Veranda Grill. Never having grilled before, I was terrified."

"Just turn it up high, close the lid and wait for it to get hot." John told me.

"That's it?" I asked.

"Pop the steaks on and close the lid. Sear them for five minutes. Turn them and close the lid again—and that's it."

Minutes later, dinner was indeed done. And that was all it took for Tonya to be sold on the idea of the Electric Veranda Grill and love the idea of grilling. Tonya now cooks on the Veranda grill with ease and confidence, partly because it's so simple and the recipes we've developed enable anyone to throw together a great mid-week dinner in no time. You'll find Tonya's favorite grilling recipes on pages 160 to 193.

Lynne admits that she's still happy to let Don do the grilling, but now that she's relinquished her role as the CFO of Masterbuilt, she has ample time to test new dessert recipes on the Electric Fryer. She's particularly fond of our signature fried pecan pies; and Don, well, he's still particularly fond of Lynne.

Continued on page 194

Top Left:
(Left to Right) Don's Family–Lynne, Brett, Trevor, Blake and Don

Top Right:
Tonya, John & Don visit THE VIEW

Bottom:
Tonya and John at QVC

 "Licensed to Grill..."
No backyard required.

For the instant gratification crowd, we've created the Masterbuilt Electric Veranda Grill. It's perfect whether you're space-starved, time-starved or simply starved. It's compact, elegant and fits comfortably on a small outdoor veranda or balcony. It assembles easily in less than 30 minutes and heats even faster. You can come home, turn it on, and open it up. Under the hood, you'll find a 200-square-inch grill rack perfect for giving hot dogs, hamburgers and even steaks that flame-grilled taste. Turn it up and you can get 1650 watts of power that you can control with ease, thanks to a temperature control gauge. No more worrying about charcoal losing heat or if there's still gas in your tank.

TIPS

- To sear the perfect steaks and burgers and lock in the juices, set the grill on high for 10 minutes and pre-heat with lid closed. Quickly open grill and place food in and immediately close lid. Sear for 3 to 5 minutes, open lid and turn food, close lid, and cook for 3 to 5 additional minutes. Open lid, turn food again, close lid and reduce temperature if needed. Continue cooking until it has reached desired internal temperature. This method of acting quickly and keeping the lid closed as much as possible will guarantee you a delicious result!

- Just like the smoker, you can prolong the life of your grill by cleaning it after each use. Keep it covered and don't forget to store the electrical cord indoors between uses.

- Just because this grill has a "high" heat setting, it's still okay to cook "low and slow." With chicken and chops, you want to sear them on both sides on high for several minutes and then turn the grill temperature down to complete the cooking process. This will give you a much juicier result.

- If using the Veranda Grill with the heat-deflector plate, you can wrap that plate with aluminum foil to make for easier cleanup.

- Coat grill rack with non-stick spray or oil before preheating to prevent food from sticking.

Salmon Sub Sandwiches

with BBQ Sauce and Coleslaw

Serves 4

BBQ Sauce:

1. In medium skillet, heat vegetable oil on medium heat, add onions and garlic, and sauté until soft. Reduce heat and add ketchup, Tabasco sauce, Worcestershire sauce, mustard, and vinegar. Cook for 2 minutes. Cool the sauce and puree in a blender. Pour into a small bowl and set sauce aside.

Coleslaw:

1. Whisk mayonnaise and vinegar in a medium bowl. Add the coleslaw mix and cilantro. Season with salt and pepper to taste, mixing coleslaw well. Refrigerate until the salmon is cooked.

Salmon:

1. Preheat grill to medium-high heat. Rub each salmon filet with vegetable oil, and sprinkle with salt and pepper. Grill the salmon skin side up for 4 minutes. Turn and brush with the BBQ sauce. Continue to grill until skin is crisp and fish is cooked through, for 6 minutes, or until the meat of the fish is opaque in color. Once salmon is done, remove and place on a platter. You may want to remove and discard the salmon skin.

2. Add the buns to the grill and toast. Once buns are toasted, place a piece of salmon on bun. Brush salmon with BBQ sauce and top with coleslaw. Serve with the leftover sauce.

JOHN *says*

Grilled salmon is as good for you as it tastes because it's high in omega oils. Preheat and lightly oil your grill before you start cooking. Start by grilling the salmon skin side up. This allows the natural fat under the skin to be drawn into the filet, keeping it rich and moist.

You'll Need:

- 4 (6 ounce) Salmon filets (skin on)
- 1 teaspoon vegetable oil
- Salt and black pepper
- 4 sub or hoagie rolls

BBQ Sauce:

- 1 tablespoon vegetable oil
- ¼ cup onion, finely minced
- 1 clove garlic, finely minced
- ½ cup ketchup
- 1 tablespoon Tabasco chipotle sauce
- 1 teaspoon Worcestershire sauce
- ½ teaspoon dry mustard
- 1 tablespoon cider vinegar

Coleslaw:

- 3 tablespoons mayonnaise
- 1 tablespoon cider vinegar
- 2 cups prepared coleslaw mix (available in your supermarket produce section)
- 1 ½ tablespoons cilantro (optional)
- Salt and black pepper

Mexican Beef Flank Steak Salad

Serves 2

Steak:

1. In a small bowl, combine all the rub ingredients and mix well. Coat the flank steak liberally on both sides. Refrigerate uncovered for 2 hours.

2. Grill steak on high heat for 8 minutes on each side, until internal temperature reaches 145° F. Remove from grill, wrap in aluminum foil, and let steak rest for 10 minutes. When the steak cools, slice into fine strips against the grain.

Dressing:

1. Combine lime juice, cilantro, sugar, chili powder, and salt in a blender, then blend at high speed. While the blender is running, add the olive oil in a slow stream until the dressing emulsifies.

Salad:

1. Place the chopped lettuce on a large platter, add sliced avocado, tomato, Cheddar cheese, black beans, and olives. Add strips of steak on top and gently mix salad while adding dressing.

JOHN says

Flank steak is typically less expensive and is great for a grilled salad because it's thin and cooks quickly. The Mexican rub complements the beefy flavor perfectly and develops a dark brown crust. Don't forget to wrap the steak in foil as it comes off the grill and let it stand for 10 minutes. The dressing lends a refreshing hint of lime that takes this dish to another level. If you like, warm some corn tortillas and turn the leftover salad into wraps that the kids will love.

You'll Need:

-   1 ½ lbs. beef flank steak

Dry Rub:

-   2 cloves garlic, finely chopped
-   1 tablespoon chili powder
-   2 teaspoons ground cumin
-   ½ teaspoon salt
-   ½ teaspoon black pepper

Dressing:

-   ¼ cup fresh lime juice
-   ½ cup fresh cilantro, chopped and stems removed
-   1 teaspoon sugar
-   1 tablespoon chili powder
-   ½ teaspoon salt
-   ½ cup extra virgin olive oil

Salad:

-   1 head romaine lettuce, chopped
-   1 firm-ripe avocado
-   1 large tomato, chopped and seeded
-   1 ½ cups extra-sharp Cheddar cheese, grated
-   1 (15 ounce) can black beans, drained and rinsed
-   ½ cup black olives, pitted and sliced, drained

GRILLED

Lamb Kabobs

Serves 4

Marinade:

1. Place the oil in a large skillet; add onion and sauté for 8 minutes or until translucent. Add garlic and cook 1 minute. Add the turmeric and curry powder, then cook 1 minute more. Stir in the brown sugar, apricot preserves, cayenne pepper, chili powder, vinegar, and buttermilk. Simmer for 10 minutes.

2. Cool the marinade and place in a large, sealable bowl.

Lamb Kabobs:

1. Add lamb to marinade mixture. Cover and marinate in refrigerator for 8 hours or overnight.

2. Preheat grill to 350° F (medium setting). Soak 4 (12-inch) wooden skewers in water for 30 minutes. Remove lamb from marinade, reserving marinade. Thread 2 to 3 pieces of lamb onto a skewer. Roll up a bacon slice, starting from a short end, then thread onto skewer. Add 2 or 3 more pieces of lamb, then another rolled bacon slice. Repeat procedure with remaining lamb and bacon using the remaining skewers. Grill at 350° F for 30 minutes, turning skewers twice, to cook evenly.

3. Place remaining marinade in a small saucepan, bring to a boil and simmer for 10 minutes. Serve over rice.

You'll Need:

- 2 lbs. lamb, cut into 1 inch cubes
- 6 strips center-cut bacon
- Skewers, soaked in water to moisten

Marinade:

- 1 tablespoon extra-virgin olive oil
- 2 medium yellow onions, chopped
- 1 clove garlic, crushed
- 1 teaspoon turmeric
- ½ teaspoon curry powder
- 2 tablespoons brown sugar
- 2 tablespoons apricot preserves
- ¼ teaspoon cayenne pepper
- ¼ teaspoon chili powder
- ½ cup apple cider vinegar
- 1 cup buttermilk
- 2 cups cooked rice

JOHN *says*

This dish is really called *Sosaties* (suh-saa-tee), a South African dish, but we just call it *"Dadgum Good* Lamb Kabobs." The secret is in the marinade; however, if time does not allow you to marinate overnight, just do so for 30 minutes to 1 hour. Remember, the longer you marinate, the better your lamb will taste.

GRILLED

Grilled Salmon
with a Creamy Horseradish Sauce
Serves 6

1. Spray grill rack generously with nonstick spray. Preheat grill on medium setting.

2. Sprinkle salmon filets with salt and pepper. In a small bowl, whisk oil, horseradish, soy sauce, and garlic. Brush oil mixture over both sides of salmon filets.

3. Place salmon on the grill and cook just until opaque in center, about 4 minutes per side. Transfer salmon to plates. Serve with sauce.

Sauce:
1. In a small bowl, combine sour cream, mayonnaise, horseradish, basil, lemon juice, and soy sauce. Season with salt and pepper. Cover and chill in refrigerator until ready to serve.

You'll Need:
- 6 (1-inch thick, 6 ounces each) salmon filets, (skin on)
- ½ teaspoon salt
- ¼ teaspoon black pepper
- ⅓ cup vegetable oil
- 1 tablespoon horseradish
- 1 tablespoon soy sauce
- 1 clove garlic, minced

Sauce:
- ¾ cup sour cream
- ¼ cup mayonnaise
- 2 tablespoons horseradish
- 2 tablespoons fresh basil, chopped
- 1 tablespoon fresh lemon juice
- 1 teaspoon soy sauce
- Salt and black pepper

JOHN *says*

I love grilled salmon, especially since it is a healthy choice. When I am watching my waistline, I use the horseradish sauce sparingly. However, it is so *Dadgum Good*, I forget about my waistline and indulge. This sauce also makes a great accompaniment to our Smoked Prime Rib. (See page 121 for recipe.)

GRILLED

You'll Need:

- 1 large red bell pepper
- 1 large yellow bell pepper
- 1 large orange bell pepper
- 1 large green bell pepper
- 4 tablespoons extra virgin olive oil
- 2 tablespoons pine nuts
- 2 cloves garlic, minced
- 2 tablespoons dried currants
- 2 tablespoons wine vinegar
- ¼ cup parsley, chopped
- ½ cup feta cheese, crumbled
- Salt and black pepper

Mediterranean Pepper Salad

Serves 2 to 3

1. Preheat grill to high heat. Grill all the peppers over high heat until the skins blister and char.

2. Remove from grill and place in a large brown paper bag to cool. When the peppers are cool enough to handle, peel and discard the charred skin, seeds and stems. Quarter the peppers lengthwise and arrange on a large serving platter.

3. In a small skillet, heat 2 tablespoons olive oil. Add pine nuts to the oil and cook over moderate heat for 3 minutes. Add minced garlic and cook for another minute. Stir in the dried currants. Remove skillet from heat and stir in the remaining 2 tablespoons of extra virgin olive oil.

4. Cool the mixture to room temperature, and whisk in the wine vinegar. Stir in the chopped parsley and crumbled feta. Season with salt and pepper. Pour the mixture over the peppers and serve immediately.

> **JOHN** *says*

Just a few minutes on the grill gives bell peppers a sweet smoky flavor. Be careful not to over roast the peppers. As soon as the skin puffs up and turns black, they're ready. You want them soft, not mushy. Also, take care not to overcook the pine nuts. You want the nuts to be sweet, not bitter. This salad never fails to impress.

Grilled Caesar Salad

Serves 4

1. Preheat grill to 350° F (medium setting).

2. To make the dressing, combine anchovies, garlic, oil, salt, and pepper in a food processor, then process on high until smooth. Add egg and lemon juice and process until combined. Makes ¾ cup dressing.

3. Brush both sides of baguette slices with dressing. Place bread slices on aluminum foil and grill, turning once, 3 to 4 minutes each side, or until toasted. Cut Romaine hearts in half lengthwise, and grill with cut sides down for 2 minutes. Do not turn. Chop Romaine crosswise into 2-inch width strips, and transfer to a medium mixing bowl. Cut the grilled baguette slices into ½-inch cubes and add to Romaine, along with the Parmigiano-Reggiano cheese. Toss and serve immediately with remaining salad dressing.

You'll Need:
- 2 flat anchovy filets, drained
- 2 cloves garlic
- ½ cup extra-virgin olive oil
- ¼ teaspoon salt
- ¼ teaspoon black pepper
- 1 large egg
- 2 tablespoons fresh lemon juice
- 12 slices baguette, sliced into 12 (½-inch) slices
- 4 Romaine hearts, halved
- 1 cup Parmigiano-Reggiano cheese, finely grated

JOHN says

I figure if people put grilled steak or chicken on their salads, why not put a salad on the grill. The lettuce ends will char, but it stays remarkably crisp and sweet. Combine that sweetness with the char-grilled flavor and you have a wonderful salad.

GRILLED

Grilled Italian Style Peppers

Serves 6

1. Peel eggplants and cut them into ¾ inch cubes. Layer them in a colander, sprinkling each layer with salt. Place the colander over a sink and let the eggplant drain for approximately one hour.

2. Spray a 13 by 9-inch baking pan with cooking spray. With a small knife, cut off the very top of the peppers, removing seeds and membranes. Stand peppers on end in the pan.

3. Preheat grill to 350° F (medium setting).

4. Rinse the drained eggplant and pat dry with paper towels. In a large skillet, heat ½ cup of oil over medium heat. Cook eggplant until tender, about 10 minutes. Stir in the tomatoes, olives, anchovies, capers, garlic, parsley, and pepper. Simmer and cook for 5 minutes. Stir in ½ cup panko and remove from heat. Stuff the peppers evenly with the eggplant mixture. Sprinkle peppers evenly with remaining ½ cup panko and drizzle with remaining 3 tablespoons olive oil. Pour 1 cup water into the pan around the peppers.

5. Grill, covered, for 1 hour until peppers are lightly browned and slightly crispy.

JOHN *says*

Anchovies, olives and capers give this dish its distinctive Italian flavor. Don't shy away from the anchovies. The salty, assertive flavor mellows out during cooking, adding richness and depth. You won't even know they're there. To maximize flavor, add the anchovies directly from their container, along with the oil. The extra oil infused with anchovy adds extra flavor.

You'll Need:

- 2 medium eggplants
- ¹⁄₁₆ teaspoon salt
- 6 large red, green, or yellow peppers (may use two of each color for colorful presentation)
- ½ cup plus 3 tablespoons extra virgin olive oil
- 3 medium tomatoes, peeled, seeded, and chopped
- 1 cup black olives, pitted
- 6 anchovy filets, finely chopped
- 3 tablespoons capers, rinsed and drained
- 1 large garlic clove, finely chopped
- 3 tablespoons fresh parsley, chopped
- ½ teaspoon black pepper
- 1 cup panko (Japanese-style bread crumbs)
- 1 cup water

Swordfish Rolls

Serves 6 to 7 as an appetizer

1. Preheat grill to 350° F (medium setting).

2. Place the swordfish slices between two sheets of plastic wrap. Using a meat pounder or a mallet, gently pound the slices evenly to ¼-inch thickness. Cut the fish into 3 x 2-inch slices. In a bowl, combine 1 cup panko, capers, parsley, garlic, salt, and pepper. Add 3 tablespoons of oil and mix until the crumbs are moistened.

3. Place a tablespoon of panko mixture at one narrow end of each piece of fish, roll the fish up around the panko and fasten it with a toothpick. Whisk together the lemon juice and the remaining 1 tablespoon olive oil. Brush the mixture over the rolls and sprinkle with remaining ½ cup panko, patting it on so that it sticks to the fish.

4. Grill the rolls at 350° F for 3 to 4 minutes on each side, until brown and rolls are firm when pressed in the center. Serve hot with lemon wedges.

You'll Need:

- 1 ½ lbs. swordfish, skin removed, cut into thin slices
- 1 ½ cups panko (Japanese-style bread crumbs)
- 2 tablespoons capers, drained and chopped
- 2 tablespoons fresh parsley, chopped
- 1 large clove garlic, minced
- ¼ teaspoon salt
- ¼ teaspoon black pepper
- 4 tablespoons extra virgin olive oil
- 2 tablespoons fresh lemon juice
- 1 large lemon, cut in wedges

JOHN says

Don and I were fishing in Mexico and it took 3 hours one day to land a swordfish. Fortunately, it took far less time to prepare this meal, with help from the locals. Cook with olive oil to help keep the fish moist and don't overcook. You won't need a few hours to catch a swordfish for this dish, but you may need a 3 hour siesta after the meal. It's that *Dadgum Good!*

GRILLED

Lemon Pepper Chicken

Serves 4 to 6

You'll Need:

- 1 (3 ½ lb.) whole chicken
- 2 tablespoons black peppercorns
- 1 tablespoon fennel seeds
- 1 cinnamon stick
- 2 cloves garlic, crushed
- 2 medium lemons, cut into wedges
- 4 tablespoons butter, melted

1. Using poultry shears, butterfly* the chicken, open it flat, and place the breast side up in a large baking dish or pan.

2. Coarsely crush peppercorns, fennel, and cinnamon in a blender. Mix with the crushed garlic and rub over the entire chicken, inside and out. Cut the lemons into wedges and squeeze juice over the chicken. Scatter the lemon pieces under and over the chicken. Marinate the chicken in refrigerator overnight in a baking dish, or resealable plastic bag.

3. Preheat the grill to 350° F (medium setting). Pour melted butter over chicken. With grill lid closed, grill chicken for 15 minutes, then turn and grill an additional 15 minutes, or until internal temperature reaches 165° F. Remove from grill, cover with aluminum foil, and let chicken stand for 10 minutes before carving and serving.

JOHN *says*

Grilled fresh vegetables make a tasty complement to this chicken dish. I like to cut zucchini in half lengthwise, coat with olive oil and sprinkle with salt and pepper. Place them on the grill alongside the chicken during the last 15 minutes of cooking time.

*Refer to page 179 for how to butterfly a chicken.

Grilled Greek Chicken Salad

Serves 2 to 4

1. In a medium bowl, combine dill, olive oil, red onion, garlic, lemon zest, lemon juice, and fennel. Place the chicken in a resealable plastic bag and marinate for 1 to 4 hours in refrigerator.

2. Preheat grill to 350° F (medium setting).

3. Remove chicken from marinade. Place chicken breasts on grill and cook 8 minutes each side.

4. Place remaining marinade in a small saucepan and bring to a boil. Baste chicken with marinade. Turn and grill another 4 minutes each side, or until the internal temperature reaches 165° F. Remove from grill, and salt and pepper to taste. Wrap in aluminum foil until cool.

Salad:

1. In a large salad bowl, combine lettuce, tomato, cucumber, red onion, feta cheese, and black olives.

2. In a food processor, combine vinegar, oregano, salt, and pepper, and mix on high. Add olive oil in a slow stream while mixing. When dressing is well mixed, lightly drizzle over the salad and toss.

3. Divide salad between plates. Top each serving with a breast of chicken.

You'll Need:

- ½ cup dill, chopped
- ¼ cup extra virgin olive oil
- 1 small red onion, sliced
- 3 cloves garlic, crushed
- Zest of one lemon
- Juice of one lemon
- 1 teaspoon crushed fennel
- 4 skinless boneless chicken breasts
- Salt and black pepper

Salad:

- 1 heart romaine lettuce
- 1 large tomato cubed
- 1 cucumber, cubed
- 1 small red onion, sliced
- 1 cup feta cheese, cubed
- 1 cup black olives
- ¼ cup red wine vinegar
- 1 ½ teaspoons dried oregano, crushed
- 1 teaspoon of salt
- ¹⁄₁₆ teaspoon of black pepper
- ¾ cup extra virgin olive oil

JOHN *says*

I love Greek and Italian salads and chicken complements this nicely. This recipe falls on the healthier side of my favorite food list.

GRILLED

Jamaican Jerk Chicken

Serves 6

1. In a food processor or blender puree the scallions, chilies, soy sauce, lime juice, allspice, mustard, bay leaves, garlic, salt, sugar, thyme, cinnamon, and olive oil.

2. Divide thighs and place in 2 heavy-duty resealable plastic bags, about 6 per bag. Spoon the marinade over the thighs, coating them well. Press out the excess air and seal the bags. Let the thighs marinate in the refrigerator for at least 24 hours, turning the bags over several times.

3. Grill the thighs on medium heat, for 10 to 15 minutes on each side, or until internal temperature reaches 165° F.

You'll Need:

- 2 cups scallions, chopped
- 2 habañera chilies, seeded
- 2 tablespoons soy sauce
- 2 tablespoons fresh lime juice
- 5 teaspoons allspice, ground
- 1 tablespoon Dijon mustard
- 2 bay leaves, crumbled and center ribs discarded
- 2 cloves garlic, crushed
- 1 tablespoon salt
- 2 teaspoons sugar
- 1 ½ teaspoons dried thyme
- 1 teaspoon cinnamon
- 1 tablespoon extra virgin olive oil
- 12 chicken thighs (bone in, skin on)

You'll Need:

- ⅓ cup sunflower oil
- 2 tablespoons toasted sesame oil
- ¼ cup pineapple juice (canned)
- 1 clove garlic
- ¼ teaspoon red pepper flakes
- 2 tablespoons soy sauce
- 1 cup fresh pineapple, cut into chunks
- 2 teaspoons freshly grated ginger
- ¼ teaspoon sea salt

Salad:

- 4 cups packed arugula
- 2 ½ cups cooked brown rice, room temperature
- 4 green onions, thinly sliced
- 3 shallots, peeled and thinly sliced
- 1 cup cashews, roasted and chopped

Pineapple Rice Salad

Serves 6

1. In a food processor or blender, combine sunflower oil, sesame oil, pineapple juice, garlic, red pepper flakes, soy sauce, fresh pineapple, ginger, and salt. Puree until smooth. Transfer to a small saucepan and gently warm just before serving. Do not simmer or boil.

2. Place arugula on a medium platter. Set aside for later.

3. In a large skillet over medium heat, combine the rice, green onions, shallots, and cashews. Add half of the dressing and sauté until heated throughout.

4. Spoon the rice mixture over the arugula and drizzle with remaining dressing. Finish with a sprinkle of green onions and cashews.

GRILLED

Lemonade Chicken

Serves 4

You'll Need:

- 1 ½ tablespoons kosher salt
- 2 tablespoons fresh rosemary
- 2 tablespoons grated lemon zest from one large lemon
- 1 teaspoon black pepper
- 3 tablespoons extra virgin olive oil
- 1 (4 ounce) can lemonade, thawed
- 1 (3 ½ to 4-lb.) whole chicken

1. Preheat grill to medium heat, 275° F to 325° F for 10 minutes and maintain temperature throughout the entire grilling process.

2. To create a rub, finely chop the salt, rosemary, and lemon zest, and mix. Add pepper.

3. Rinse and dry the chicken. Carefully loosen the skin of the chicken using a knife, or your hands, to evenly distribute the rub under the skin of the chicken. Brush the chicken with the olive oil. Halve the lemon and squeeze both halves over the chicken.

4. Open the can of lemonade and pour out ¼ cup, leaving the rest in the can. Place the lemonade can inside the chicken cavity and place the chicken upright on the grill. Grill for 30 minutes then carefully remove the can and turn the chicken over, and grill for an additional 35 minutes or until the internal temperature reaches 165° F.

5. Remove chicken from grill, wrap in aluminum foil, and let it rest for 10 minutes. Carve and serve.

JOHN *says*

The lemonade can does two jobs in this recipe. It serves as a vertical roaster while the chicken sits on it and it creates steam as the chicken grills. As a result you get a chicken with crisp skin that's incredibly moist on the inside and golden crisp on the outside. To top it off, the lemon and rosemary rub delivers an unbeatable marriage of flavors.

Lime Chicken

Serves 6 to 8

1. Place chicken in a large dish and sprinkle breasts with salt. In a medium bowl, mix corn oil, lime juice, onion, tarragon, and Tabasco. Pour over chicken breasts; marinate for 8 hours or overnight in the refrigerator.

2. Remove chicken from marinade and place on grill. Grill on medium to high heat, until done approximately 5 minutes each side or until the internal temperature reaches 165° F.

You'll Need:

- 10 to 12 boneless chicken breasts
- 2 ½ teaspoons salt
- 1 (32 ounce) bottle corn oil
- 1 (32 ounce) bottle lime juice
- 5 tablespoons chopped onion
- 5 teaspoons tarragon
- 1 ½ teaspoons Tabasco sauce

JOHN *says*

Lime gets top billing in this recipe, but the real star is the tarragon and there's a reason so many chefs favor it. The leaves are sweetly aromatic with hints of pine and anise. The flavor is distinctive with a sweetish aftertaste. To dial up the flavor, use more tarragon leaves bound together with twine as a basting brush.

GRILLED

Piri-Piri Chicken

Serves 4

1. Rinse the chicken, butterfly*, and set aside. Melt the butter in a saucepan. Combine with the olive oil, lemon juice, hot sauce, paprika, ground coriander, garlic, scallions, parsley, ginger, bay leaves, salt, and pepper in a blender and puree until smooth. Reserve half the marinade and refrigerate. Marinate the chicken with the remaining marinade and refrigerate for a minimum of 4 to 5 hours.

2. Place reserved, refrigerated marinade in a small saucepan and warm over a low heat. Heat the grill to 425° F (high setting). Place chicken breast side-up on the grill. Baste with the marinade and close grill lid for 15 minutes. Reduce heat to low and cook for another 45 minutes with the grill lid closed, or until internal temperature reaches 165° F. Baste the chicken generously, then carefully flip the chicken over to brown the skin for 5 to 10 minutes. Remove chicken from grill, wrap in foil, and allow to rest for 5 minutes. Carve chicken and place in a serving dish. Drizzle with warm leftover marinade. Serve with rice and pass around the remaining marinade as a sauce.

*How to Butterfly a Chicken

You'll need a cutting board, a good sharp knife, and poultry shears. Using the poultry shears, cut along either side of the backbone, removing it completely. Turn the chicken over and lay it out; press into the middle to break the wishbone. Flip the chicken over again and cut away the membrane holding the meat to the keel bone. Slide your thumbs up both sides of the keel bone to loosen the meat from it. Use your poultry shears to cut the end of the keel bone from the chicken and remove it. It's easier than it sounds.

You'll Need:

- 1 (3 ½ lb.) whole chicken
- 4 tablespoons salted butter
- ½ cup extra-virgin olive oil
- ½ cup fresh lemon juice
- 4 tablespoons Tabasco (or habañero sauce if you like it hot!)
- 1 tablespoon paprika
- 1 teaspoon ground coriander
- 3 cloves garlic, chopped
- 3 scallions, chopped
- 3 tablespoons fresh parsley, chopped
- 1 ½ teaspoons fresh ginger root, chopped
- 2 bay leaves crumbled
- 1 teaspoon salt
- ½ teaspoon black pepper

JOHN *says*

Piri-piri literally means "chilly-chilly" in Swahili. For me, it just means hot-hot and *Dadgum-Dadgum Good!* By the way, you may be able to find the piri-piri sauce at your local supermarket.

GRILLED

Beef Sirloin
with Pepper and Cinnamon
Serves 4

You'll Need:

- 4 (8 ounce) beef sirloin steaks, 1-inch thick
- 1 teaspoon salt
- 1 tablespoon black pepper
- ½ teaspoon cinnamon, ground
- 2 tablespoons butter, melted

Sauce:
- 2 teaspoons butter
- $\frac{1}{16}$ teaspoon cinnamon
- $\frac{1}{16}$ teaspoon black pepper
- ⅔ cup regular whipping cream
- 4 tablespoons shallots, finely chopped

1. Preheat grill to 350° F (medium setting).

2. Allow steaks to stand at room temperature at least 15 minutes before cooking. Sprinkle both sides of steaks with salt, pepper, and cinnamon.

3. Grill steaks for 5 minutes on each side, or until internal temperature reaches 145° F. Remove steaks from grill; drizzle with 2 tablespoons of melted butter and wrap in aluminum foil. Let steaks rest for 5 minutes before serving.

Sauce:

1. Mix butter, cinnamon, pepper, cream, and shallots in small saucepan. Bring to a simmer, stirring well. Serve with steaks as a sauce.

JOHN says

Growing up, I thought cinnamon was only used on toast in the mornings for breakfast. I found that crushing cinnamon together with black pepper creates a unique rub for steaks. Now I can enjoy the taste of cinnamon at dinnertime, too. I once tried to make the rub work on my morning toast, and let's just say it's best on a steak!

Flank Steak
with Chimichurri Sauce
Serves 4

1. Using a food processor or blender, combine garlic cloves, black pepper, paprika, chili flakes, red grape juice, olive oil, parsley leaves, oregano, and salt. Blend until smooth.

2. Score the flank steak with a fork to allow the marinade to penetrate the meat. Place the meat in a resealable plastic bag with half of the marinade, and refrigerate for 4 hours. Chill remaining marinade for 4 hours in a separate container.

3. Grill the flank steak over medium heat 8 minutes per side, or until internal temperature reaches 145° F. Remove from the grill and wrap in foil. Let steak rest for 5 minutes before cutting. Slice the flank steak against the grain in long, thin cuts.

4. Warm reserved marinade in a small saucepan over low heat, and drizzle over the meat before serving.

You'll Need:
- 8 cloves garlic, minced
- 2 teaspoons black pepper
- 2 teaspoons paprika
- 1 teaspoon hot chili flakes
- ⅔ cup red grape juice
- ½ cup extra virgin olive oil
- 2 cups parsley leaves, finely chopped
- 4 teaspoons dried oregano
- 1 teaspoon salt
- 1 ½ lbs. beef flank steak

JOHN says

Flank steak and skirt steak are not the same cut of meat, but they come from the same general area of the cow—the flank area between the ribs and hip. The flank steak is the traditional cut used for a London Broil. It is long, thin, and full of tough connective tissue, and is, therefore, usually marinated before being broiled or grilled whole. Because it is tough, you usually slice it thinly on a diagonal across the grain to sever the tough fibers and make the flavorful steak more chewable.

Chicken Kabobs
with Grilled Corn and Tomato Salad
Serves 4

1. Preheat the grill to 300° F (low to medium setting).

2. In a medium bowl, add chicken, garlic, thyme, olive oil, salt, and pepper. Toss until well coated. Cover and refrigerate for 20 to 30 minutes.

3. Thread chicken onto skewers. Place kabobs and corn on the grill and cook for 10 minutes. Turn and cook another 10 minutes, or until corn is starting to show char marks.

Salad:

1. In a medium bowl, add the tomatoes, scallions, olive oil, vinegar, salt, and pepper. Toss until well coated. Serve with chicken and corn.

You'll Need:
- 1 ½ boneless skinless chicken breasts, cut into 2-inch cubes
- 2 cloves garlic, finely chopped
- 1 tablespoon fresh thyme
- 2 tablespoons extra virgin olive oil
- ½ teaspoon kosher salt
- ½ teaspoon black pepper
- 4 ears of corn, husks removed
- 8 skewers, soaked in water to moisten

Salad:
- 1 pint grape tomatoes, halved
- 2 scallions, chopped
- 1 tablespoon extra virgin olive oil
- 1 tablespoon balsamic vinegar
- ¾ teaspoon kosher salt
- ¾ teaspoon black pepper

JOHN *says*

You can leave the husk on the corn while grilling if you would like. Once you see the shape of the kernels burning through the husk, your corn is about ready. If you grill with indirect heat, you will need to grill for about 1 hour. Put corn on grill first, then the kabobs.

Herbed Tuna Burgers
with Olive Spread

Serves 6

1. In a large bowl, combine tuna, capers, shallots, mustard, thyme, rosemary, salt, and pepper. Shape tuna mixture into 6 (¾-inch thick) patties and place on a plate. Cover and refrigerate for 1 hour.

2. Spray grill rack with nonstick spray. Preheat grill to 350° F (medium setting). Place burgers on grill and cook 4 minutes per side, until internal temperature reaches 145° F.

3. Arrange bread bottoms; spread with olive spread. Top each with burger, tomato, onion, and arugula.

Olive Spread:

1. In a mini food processor, puree the olives, olive oil, shallots, mint, thyme, and lemon juice. Season olive spread with salt and pepper.

You'll Need:

- 2 lbs. fresh tuna steaks, finely diced and chilled
- 2 tablespoons capers, drained and chopped
- 2 tablespoons shallots, chopped
- 1 tablespoon Dijon mustard
- 1 teaspoon fresh thyme, minced
- 1 teaspoon fresh rosemary, minced
- ¾ teaspoon coarse kosher salt
- 1 teaspoon black pepper
- 6 (4-inch) rolls or herb focaccia bread
- 1 large tomato, sliced
- 1 medium onion, thinly sliced
- 2 cups baby arugula

Olive Spread:

- 1 cup dark purple olives, pitted
- 3 tablespoons extra-virgin olive oil
- 2 tablespoons shallots, chopped
- 2 tablespoons fresh mint, chopped
- 2 teaspoons fresh thyme, chopped
- 2 teaspoons fresh lemon juice
- Salt and black pepper

JOHN says

To keep your burgers moist, choose the freshest tuna you can find and consider serving them medium-rare to medium – don't overcook. Using this olive spread definitely does the trick for making these *Dadgum Good!*

GRILLED

Balsamic Pork Chops

Serves 4

1. Mix the oil, vinegar, and rosemary. Season the chops with salt and pepper. Coat the chops evenly with the oil mixture. Let the chops stand at room temperature while the grill heats.

2. Set grill to medium, approximately 350° F. Grill chops 10 minutes per side, or until internal temperature reaches 160° F.

You'll Need:

- 2 tablespoons extra virgin olive oil
- 2 tablespoons balsamic vinegar
- 1 tablespoon fresh rosemary, minced
- 4 (1-inch thick) pork chops, bone-in or boneless
- Salt and black pepper

JOHN *says*

Although I enjoy thick-cut pork chops, some people like them thinner. With either cut you use, be sure not to overcook the pork. Timing is everything… lock in those juices, don't cook' em out!

GRILLED

Caribbean Kabobs
Serves 4 to 6

You'll Need:

- 2 lbs. boneless chicken breasts, cut into 1 ½ inch cubes
- ½ cup plantains, green, cut into 1 ½ inch pieces
- 4 cups papaya, cut into 1 ½ inch pieces
- 3 cups pineapple, cut into 1 ½ inch pieces
- Skewers, soaked in water to moisten

Marinade:

- 1 fresh mango, peeled, cored and pureed
- 3 tablespoons fresh lime juice
- 2 tablespoons shallots, finely chopped
- 2 tablespoons brown sugar, firmly packed
- 2 tablespoons extra virgin olive oil
- 1 tablespoon curry powder
- 1 tablespoon garlic paste
- ½ teaspoon cayenne pepper
- ½ teaspoon salt

1. Preheat grill to 300° F (low to medium heat).

2. In a non-reactive bowl, combine pureed mango, with lime juice, shallots, brown sugar, olive oil, curry powder, garlic paste, cayenne pepper, and salt. Add chicken pieces, toss well to marinate, and refrigerate 8 hours, or overnight.

3. Drain marinade from chicken into a small saucepan. Cook over medium heat, stirring often, for 3 to 5 minutes. Set aside for basting chicken during grilling.

4. Thread 4 to 5 chicken pieces onto each skewer, alternating chicken with plantains, papaya, and pineapple pieces. Grill on medium heat for 5 to 7 minutes per side, occasionally brushing kabobs with reserved marinade.

JOHN *says*

Though this kabob recipe call for skinless chicken breast, you can also use dark meat from the thigh. Whatever you choose, don't thread the white and dark meat onto the same kabob, they cook at different rates and your kabobs will be unevenly cooked.

Kansas City-Style BBQ Chicken

Serves 3 to 6

1. In a large saucepan over medium heat, warm the canola oil. Add the onions and garlic, then sauté, stirring occasionally, until the onions are caramelized and very tender, about 12 to 15 minutes.

2. Add the tomatoes, ketchup, brown sugar, corn syrup, Worcestershire sauce, molasses, vinegar, mustard, red pepper flakes, and paprika. Bring to a simmer, then reduce heat to medium-low and cook, stirring occasionally, until the sauce is thickened, 45 minutes to an hour. Season with salt and black pepper.

3. Heat grill to high.

4. Season the chicken with salt and black pepper. Arrange the chicken on the grill and cook about 8 minutes, turning frequently with tongs to prevent scorching. Using half the sauce, baste the chicken, turning often to baste with more sauce, for an additional 8 to 10 minutes.

5. Serve immediately with remaining sauce.

You'll Need:

- ¼ cup canola oil
- 2 yellow onions, diced (3 cups)
- 4 cloves garlic, minced
- 2 cups tomatoes, seeded and diced
- ½ cup ketchup
- ½ cup light brown sugar, firmly packed
- ¼ cup light corn syrup
- 2 tablespoons Worcestershire sauce
- ¼ cup molasses
- ½ cup cider vinegar
- ¼ cup Dijon mustard
- ½ teaspoon red pepper flakes
- 1 tablespoon paprika
- 1 (3 ½ lb.) chicken, cut into 8 pieces
- Salt and black pepper to taste

JOHN says

The secret to juicy chicken is in the grilling method. If you prefer "low-and-slow," you can let it go and not turn as frequently. If you like to grill "hot-and-fast," you'll need to babysit the chicken and turn more often. Do not overcook, which will give you a dry result. Complement this chicken dish with our steamed Sweet Corn with Cilantro Chili Butter. (See page 82 for recipe.)

GRILLED

Beef or Chicken Fajitas

Serves 4

Marinade:

1. Combine garlic, salt, cumin, chili powder, crushed red pepper, oil, and lemon juice in a medium-size bowl.

Fajitas:

1. Score skin of beef or chicken with cross-hatched, diamond-shaped marks and rub meat with marinade. Refrigerate for at least 2 hours.

2. Preheat grill to 350° F (medium heat).

3. Place onion, green onion, and green and red peppers in aluminum foil and add olive oil. Seal foil and place on grill for 7 minutes, then remove and set aside. Grill beef or chicken for 5 to 8 minutes, or until internal temperature of chicken reaches 165° F, or beef temperature reaches 160° F. Remove from heat, wrap in foil, and let rest for 5 minutes. When ready to serve, slice beef or chicken into strips and transfer to bowl with the juices. Serve with warm corn tortillas, grilled onion mixture, avocado, hot sauce, salsa, sour cream and or freshly chopped tomatoes.

You'll Need:
- 1 clove garlic
- 1 ½ teaspoons salt
- 1 ½ teaspoons ground cumin
- 1 teaspoon chili powder
- ½ teaspoon crushed red pepper
- 2 tablespoons vegetable oil
- 2 tablespoons lemon juice
- 1 ½ lbs. flank or New York strip steak, or chicken breast
- 3 tablespoons olive oil
- 1 cup yellow onion, sliced
- ½ cup green onion, sliced
- 1 cup green bell pepper, sliced
- 1 cup red bell pepper, sliced
- 8 medium corn tortillas

JOHN says

Here's a mid-week dinner that comes together on the grill fast. Chicken and beef both make fine fajitas. You may want to stay away from skirt steak, which can be tough, and opt for flank steak instead. Grilling the vegetables in the aluminum foil with oil prevents them from falling through the grill grates.

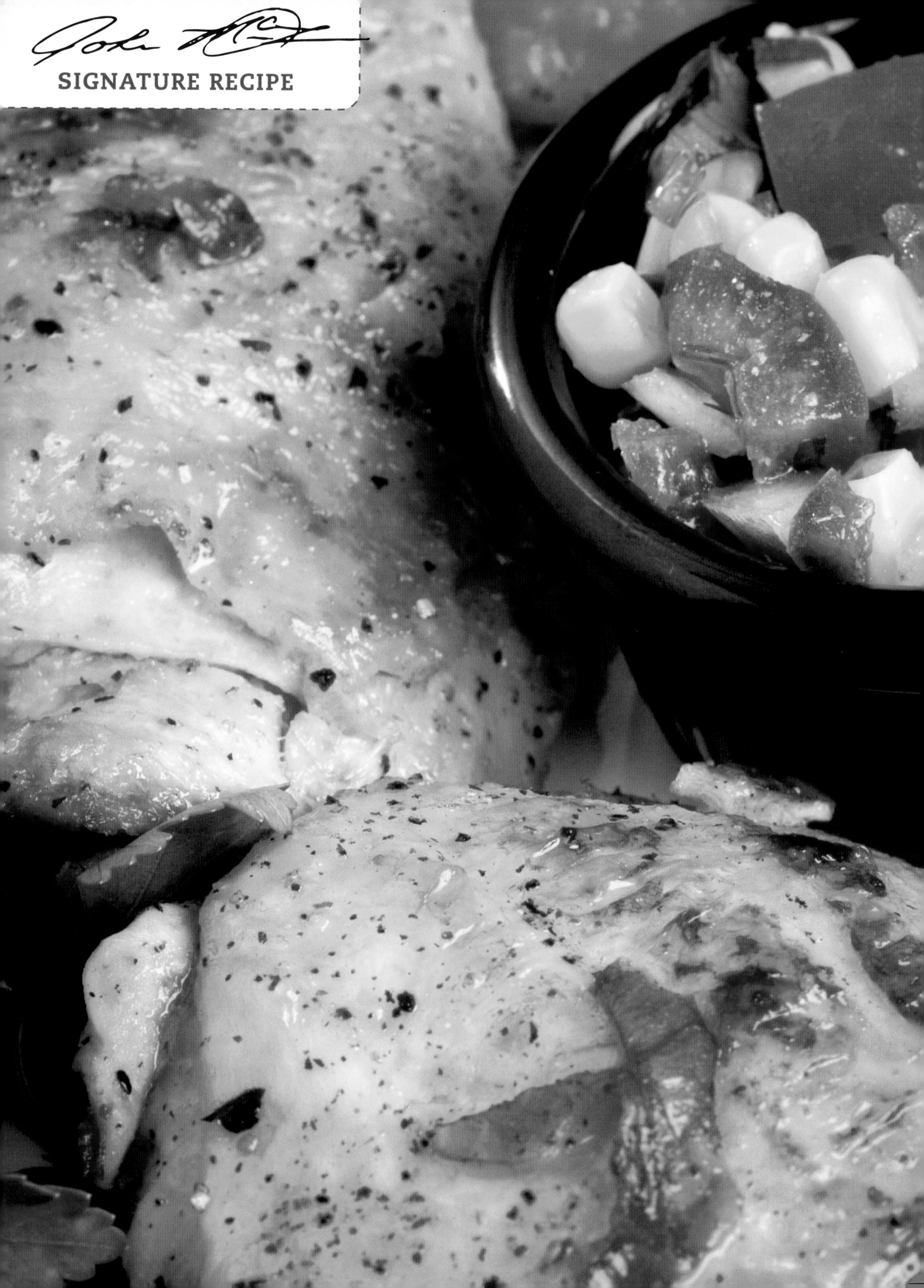
SIGNATURE RECIPE

Chicken Thighs
with Avocado and Tomato Salsa
Serves 4 to 6

1. Place chicken thighs in a resealable plastic bag. Add red onion, lemon zest, ground cumin, lemon juice, and olive oil. Seal and marinate in refrigerator for 3 to 6 hours. Occasionally, turn bag to spread marinade evenly.

2. Set grill to 380° F (medium to high setting). Remove chicken from marinade. Sprinkle chicken with salt and pepper. In a small saucepan, bring marinade to a boil.

3. Grill chicken for 12 minutes per side or until internal temperature reaches 165° F, basting occasionally with marinade. Remove from grill and seal in aluminum foil.

Salsa:

1. In a medium bowl, mix the corn, tomato, red onion, cilantro, olive oil, lemon juice, cumin, and jalapeño.

2. Peel, pit and dice avocado. Add to salsa and season with salt and pepper.

3. Serve chicken with salsa on the side.

You'll Need:
- 4 lbs. chicken thighs, skins on
- ¼ cup red onion, chopped
- 1 tablespoon grated lemon zest
- 1 teaspoon ground cumin
- ¼ cup fresh lemon juice
- 3 tablespoons olive oil
- Salt and black pepper to taste

Salsa:
- 1 cup fresh corn kernels
- 1 large tomato, seeded and diced
- ⅔ cup red onion, chopped
- ½ cup cilantro, chopped
- 2 tablespoons olive oil
- 1 tablespoon fresh lemon juice
- ½ teaspoon cumin
- 1 jalapeño pepper, seeded and minced
- 1 avocado
- Salt and black pepper

JOHN *says*

Here's one time when cheaper is actually better. Chicken thighs may be one of the cheaper cuts, but you'll find they do great on the grill. Thighs are more flavorful and the extra fat in the skin makes them better suited to grilling. Some folks like to brine their chicken, but this marinade gives it all the juice it needs to make it *Dadgum Good.*

Maple BBQ Pork Burgers

Serves 4

1. Preheat grill to 350° F (medium setting).

2. Gently mix sausage and bell pepper in a medium-sized mixing bowl. Form into 4 (½-inch thick) patties, cover and refrigerate. Combine BBQ sauce, maple syrup, and cider vinegar. Reserve ½ cup sauce for basting patties on grill.

3. Remove patties from refrigerator and grill at 350° F for 5 minutes on each side. Baste one side with sauce and grill for 5 minutes then flip and baste other side, grilling for 5 minutes more, or until internal temperature reaches 160° F. Place bottoms and tops of buns on grill rack and grill for 2 minutes. Place burgers on the bottom half of the roll. Top each burger with ¼ cup coleslaw. Serve with remaining sauce. If you like, top with a pineapple slice.

You'll Need:

- 1 lb. spicy pork breakfast sausage
- 1 cup green bell pepper, diced
- 1⅓ cups of your favorite BBQ sauce
- 3 tablespoons maple syrup
- 3 tablespoons apple cider vinegar
- 8 Hawaiian rolls
- 1 cup packaged, coleslaw
- 4 pineapple slices, optional

JOHN *says*

This recipe gives you a great way to add some WOW factor to burger night. The spicy and sweet flavors blend well together. While the grill is hot, we recommend you make some extra and serve them up with a side order of eggs and hot biscuits for breakfast.

GRILLED

The Masterbuilt Story
as told by John McLemore

Don and I believe we have created the safest and best way to deep fry a turkey. So it seemed only logical that we'd make a perfect match with the famous Butterball brand. So we did what made the best sense and contacted the Butterball® Turkey Talk-Line® and offered to demonstrate the Masterbuilt Indoor Turkey Fryer in action.

I like to think of Butterball Turkey Talk-Line as the experts when it comes to turkey knowledge. Every year around the holidays, their phone lines are busy with callers looking for advice on how to prepare and cook a turkey. The Butterball team knew all the answers, but when it came to deep frying turkey they were interested in learning more. This was obviously an opportunity for us to work together.

Top:
1990 Don and John filming a cooking segment

Beside:
John and Don smoking ribs at the lake

Bottom Left:
Don and John wrap up another day of cooking

Bottom Right:
John and daughter, Bailey, get ready to eat

The trend of deep frying turkeys as a method of preparation had been growing, and in addition to providing expert cooking advice, Butterball recognized that by endorsing the Masterbuilt product line they could help consumers prepare turkey in a safe, more convenient way. To make a long story short Butterball became the first brand to officially license a deep fryer made with the expertise of Masterbuilt. The Butterball Indoor Electric Turkey Fryer was introduced in 2008 and there's been no looking back since. The brands were indeed a perfect match–combining our quality products to provide a solution to the consumer.

In fact, our deep fried Cajun turkey was selected to be presented at a ribbon cutting ceremony at the Butterball Corporate Headquarters. I must say I was really proud of our team that day. It was a highlight in the history of Masterbuilt.

Top Left:
John in New York with Fox & Friends fans.

Middle:
Don and Lynne at the lake

Top Right:
Don and John cooking on the Veranda Grill

Ashley Hatcher, inventor of the non-slip LAPPER TRAYS with John and Don. We purchased Ashley's company in 2009, and it became a part of the Masterbuilt family.

Top Left:
John and Don's family preparing to eat

Top Right:
Don and John prepared turkey for the family

Bottom Left:
Don and John, just being goofy

Bottom Right:
Paula Deen and husband, Michael, with John and his family

But the story doesn't end here. In fact, this is where it starts. With this collection of *"Dadgum Good"* McLemore recipes, every single one has been developed and tested exhaustively on our Masterbuilt products. More importantly, they've earned the approval of the McLemore family, including the very same folks who watched Don and me turn out a perfect Thanksgiving turkey nearly thirty years ago.

We're pretty certain you're going to enjoy our first collection of recipes and we look forward to your response. After all, we've grown our company by listening to customers like you, and that's how we're going to keep building it. (Follow us on Facebook and Twitter. *See our website www.dadgumthatsgood.com for links.*)

You don't have to be a professional chef to master these recipes for frying, steaming, boiling, smoking and grilling, but you'll find them really simple to master using Masterbuilt products.

Don't take our word for it. After all, the truth is in the tasting. We're confident that as you try our recipes, we will have you saying, *"Dadgum That's Good!"*

John & Mike Huckabee after an appearance on FOX & Friends

"I met John at Fox News in New York. After seeing him deep frying turkeys in his Butterball® Indoor Electric Turkey Fryer, I knew I had to get one. Not only was the turkey absolutely perfectly delicious, but the ease, convenience and foolproof manner of maintaining the ideal cooking temperature had me sold. When mine arrived, I hurried to the store, bought a 12 pound turkey, got it all injected with the Butterball® Cajun Seasoning and got ready to cook right on my kitchen counter. My wife came in and asked me what I was doing, and I explained, "frying a turkey." She reminded me that turkeys have to be fried outside, but I told her this unit was designed for indoors. The result was not only the best tasting turkey I've ever prepared, but the absolute easiest way to cook one. Even my wife was impressed with my not making a mess and the turkey being the best ever. I have been frying turkeys for years the old way with propane, temperature gauges, non stop attending the turkey and cooker and the challenge of cleaning it all up afterwards. This cooker is amazing—not only to fry turkeys, but to steam vegetables, seafood, anything. I liked it so much that I bought several others and sent to friends who loved to fry turkeys. I wanted them to keep their marriages together and have a foolproof way of preparing the turkey. I love this thing and love the fact that John has written a fantastic cookbook with recipes that are *Dadgum Good!*"

—Mike Huckabee, Fox News

Acknowledgements

The best part about writing this cookbook was having the chance to reflect back on my life with a renewed sense of gratitude to all of those who led me to this point. I'm thankful to God for all of the blessings in my life, personally and professionally. I'm incredibly grateful to my wife, Tonya, and my three children – Brooke, John and Bailey – for their unending support and love. Thanks to my parents, Dawson and Evelyn McLemore. Momma was a constant source of encouragement, and Dad gave Don and me an awesome opportunity to grow our family business. I want to thank my brother Don and his wife, Lynne, with their three boys – Blake, Brett and Trevor. Don and I always shared the priorities of God first, family second, and then business. With these shared priorities we want to say thank you to all our employees and their families, which have made Masterbuilt a success. I also want to thank Lisa Johnson, my assistant, for her invaluable help throughout the process of developing this cookbook. Lastly, I want to thank you for taking this journey with us. I look forward to hearing your stories of making *Dadgum Good* food!

Recipe Index

BOILED

SMOKED

GRILLED